"As a grieving student, your life feels like ⟨ emotions that often you can't put a name situation, and pain. This book sorts through everything I've felt, helping me feel understood. Rather than trying to show me how to stop grieving or stop experiencing these emotions, this book helps me through the grief journey, reminding me that it is important to feel for and love the person you lost in order to find healing."

—*Melanie Wolff, University of Pennsylvania student, Class of 2016*

"I see *We Get It* as a much-needed tool for those who work with college students on a daily basis. College student personnel such as clinicians, residential life staff, Dean of Student staff, and faculty and administrators could truly benefit from reading about the themes noted—and even more powerfully from the students' stories. The range of student experience covered through the first-person and beautifully honest narratives allows for a deeper level of understanding and perspective-taking, providing a unique insight into how best to support grieving students."

—*Philip M. Meilman, PhD, Director, Counseling and Psychiatric Service, and Professor, Department of Psychiatry, Georgetown University*

"Whether you're a counselor, parent, or grieving college student, the 33 stories shared here will provide insight into some of the commonalities and differences young adults experience after the death of a parent or sibling, as well as tips on how to be helpful. Their journeys of struggle and healing offer wisdom and hope."

—*Donna L. Schuurman, EdD, FT, Chief Executive Officer, The Dougy Center for Grieving Children and Families*

"This book is important. It brings to life in clear, plain English stories of young adults who have coped with the death(s) of persons they love. Heather and David get it. They understand what coping with loss entails for a college student. They make the myriad experiences of young adults dealing with bereavement come alive for all of us. The stories told by grieving young adults illustrate clearly several important themes that scholars have uncovered about bereavement. Heather and David's mastery of what they know will help others to get what the bereaved college student knows."

—*David E. Balk, Professor and Chair, Department of Health and Nutrition Sciences, Brooklyn College of the City University of New York, and author,* Helping the Bereaved College Student *of related interest*

Still Here with Me
Teenagers and Children on Losing a Parent
Edited by Suzanne Sjöqvist
ISBN 978 1 84310 501 5
eISBN 978 1 84642 580 6

Effective Grief and Bereavement Support
The Role of Family, Friends, Colleagues,
Schools and Support Professionals
Atle Dyregrov and Kari Dyregrov
ISBN 978 1 84310 667 8
eISBN 978 1 84642 833 3

Talking with Bereaved People
An Approach for Structured
and Sensitive Communication
Dodie Graves
ISBN 978 1 84310 988 4
eISBN 978 0 85700 162 7

Setting Up and Facilitating
Bereavement Support Groups
A Practical Guide
Dodie Graves
ISBN 978 1 84905 271 9
eISBN 978 0 85700 573 1

Writing in Bereavement
A Creative Handbook
Jane Moss
ISBN 978 1 84905 212 2
eISBN 978 0 85700 450 5

WE
GET
IT

Voices of Grieving College Students and Young Adults

HEATHER L. SERVATY-SEIB
AND DAVID C. FAJGENBAUM

With contributions by 33 inspirational young adults

Jessica Kingsley *Publishers*
London and Philadelphia

First published in 2015
by Jessica Kingsley Publishers
73 Collier Street
London N1 9BE, UK
and
400 Market Street, Suite 400
Philadelphia, PA 19106, USA

www.jkp.com

Library of Congress Cataloging in Publication Data
Servaty-Seib, Heather L. (Heather Lynn)
  We get it : voices of grieving college students and young adults / Heather L. Servaty-
Seib and David C.
Fajgenbaum ; with contributions by 33 inspirational young adults.
     pages cm
  Includes bibliographical references.
  ISBN 978-1-84905-752-3 (alk. paper)
  1. Grief. 2. Death. 3. Young adults--Psychology. 4. College students--Psychology.
I. Fajgenbaum, David
C. II. Title.
  BF575.G7S44 2015
  155.9'370842--dc23

                    2014048996

British Library Cataloguing in Publication Data
A CIP catalogue record for this book is available from the British Library

ISBN 978 1 84905 752 3
eISBN 978 0 85700 977 7

This book is purchased in memory of

_____

This book is dedicated to:

Anne Marie Fajgenbaum, for her beautiful life that inspired the creation of a nonprofit to help grieving college students.

Linda Ann Moline, for her passion, presence, and courage to live her own way—even at the end of her life.

David's family and friends, including Caitlin Fajgenbaum, Gena Combs, Lisa Fajgenbaum, David M. Fajgenbaum, Ben Chesson, Kiri Thompson, and David Balk.

Heather's family, including Broc, Klara, and Mia Seib.

Contents

Introduction

I feel like I'm the only person on a campus of 20,000 students who is dealing with grief, and I feel completely alone. How come no one gets it? I need support from someone who gets what I'm going through.

This is a question that both of us are frequently asked by students and a question that we asked when we were in college too. Losing a loved one is difficult at any age, but there are certain things about young adulthood that can make it a particularly difficult time, including developmental (e.g., identity development, separation/connection with family) and setting-based (e.g., geographic distance, college as fun) challenges. These unique issues often leave college students and young adults feeling unable to discuss their grief experiences and can lead to a growing sense of isolation, of being different, and pressure to pretend that everything is OK. Grieving college students can begin to believe they are the only ones in their social circles or even campuses who have experienced the illness and/or death of someone close to them and that there is no one around them who "gets" what they are going through.

These are several of the reasons that we, Heather and David, have both dedicated much of our lives to helping grieving college students and young adults. Heather has published bereavement research, advocated for young adult grievers as the President of the Association for Death Education and Counseling, and helped to establish one of the only student bereavement leave policies in the United States on her campus at Purdue University. She has also counseled many students (and parents of students) seeking support, and guided many colleagues wishing to help their grieving students. David established a peer-led grief support group at Georgetown University after his mother died, grew the organization into a national movement that has reached more than 3000 grieving students on more than 200 campuses, and helped to make college student grief a priority issue in higher education in the United States (U.S.).

Four years ago, we connected through our mutual concern for all of the students not being reached by David's nonprofit and not benefiting from Heather's research and outreach. We had seen the impact that can be made on grieving young people's lives when they receive the support they desperately need, and we knew there were many more around the world in need of support and of connection with others who "get it." Some individuals manage to find and connect with those with similar loss experiences, whereas others never do. We hope this book will help all.

We decided to assemble a book of autobiographical narratives written *by* grieving college students and young adults *for* grieving college students and young adults. We hope this book will help students and young adults to realize that they are not alone and that there are many others going through similar experiences. We believe these narratives can give readers a voice and the courage to share their grief experiences with others. We have discovered that one of the most powerful experiences for grieving individuals is to hear even a small element of their own experience being expressed by another. We wanted to make this experience possible for all regardless of their access to others with similar experiences. This book provides a window into the many grief reactions and mourning approaches of 33 grieving students and young adults; anyone who purchases this book can now read their personal stories. We have offered the whole narratives, organized them based on themes, provided commentary throughout, and reflection questions at the end of each chapter, to help grievers to keep actively moving forward. The book is primarily focused on the experience of grief during college, but several of our authors experienced a death before college and/or wrote their narrative after college. We chose to include a variety of perspectives and to provide commentary related to young adult grief outside of the college campus, so that this book could serve as a resource for young adults not currently in college.

The young adults who contributed their stories to this book wanted to make a difference in the lives of future grieving students through sharing their stories—through showing that they "get it." Rather than providing a prescription for how grief *should* be expressed, they genuinely describe the thoughts, feelings, and behaviors they experienced throughout their grief journeys. The power of this book is in the candid, engaging, and heartfelt sharing contained in these stories.

If you are a grieving college student or young adult, know that you will find multiple points of connection as you read. Keep in mind that there will also be elements contained here that are *not* part of your experience and that is OK and to be expected. Grief unfolds uniquely for each person.

This book was also written to offer guidance to those who want to support grieving college students and young adults, including family members, friends, counselors, professors, or university staff members. These individuals play vital roles in the lives of grieving young people. Reading the stories included here can provide helpful insights into the unique and dynamic nature of grief. There is not one way to grieve or mourn and we believe that message comes through clearly in these pages. If you are someone (e.g., parent, friend, counselor) who is seeking to be a supportive presence in the life of a grieving college student, know that you will gain a clearer picture of the vast range of reactions that college students experience in the face of their grief. You will leave wiser and better able to acknowledge, normalize, and facilitate the grief of these young adults.

As someone passionate about supporting grieving individuals, and who dedicates the majority of her academic and clinical efforts to encouraging and empowering young people in their grief journeys, Heather always wanted to assemble a resource for grieving college students. But, over time, she realized that grieving college students did not want or need a book that she, as a counseling psychologist and professor, would write for them! Rather, what students and young adults need is to hear the stories of their peers and to know that they are not the only one who feels/felt torn, lost, transformed, newly determined about life, etc. Heather believes this book will make a true difference, and she is proud of David and every single young adult who contributed to this volume. All of the authors have decided to take a risk—through being open about their own experiences—to allow others to know they are not alone.

David's motivation for this book is very closely tied to his own experience grieving the death of his mother during college and his desire to continue to honor her beautiful life:

My mom was the most generous and kind person I have ever known. She was the ultimate supporter—always there to listen to anyone who needed it. She began experiencing severe headaches just before it was time for me to leave home for college at Georgetown University in the summer of 2003. Initially, our family was not concerned, because we thought that she was just stressed about me, her youngest child "lil' Dave," leaving home. Two weeks after I began my freshman year, we found out that her headaches were being caused by Grade IV brain cancer. I was devastated. I couldn't understand how someone as incredible as her could deserve something like cancer. I struggled with deciding whether to return home or stay at school. She really wanted me to stay at school, and I agreed as long as I could make the four-hour drive home each weekend to see her. So I started my pre-med program constantly worrying about my mother's health and feeling completely alone. I had a couple of close friends that I told about my mom's illness, but I kept all of my emotions to myself. The three feelings that I felt over and over again were loneliness, helplessness, and guilt for being at college. Any time that I smiled or laughed, I would remember what my mom was going through. I wished that I had others to talk to. I knew I could speak to a counselor, but I believed that what I really needed was to speak to other students going through the same experience that I was.

At the start of my sophomore year, my mom's cancer returned, and she was placed in hospice care. I continued to travel home every weekend and was very lucky to have the most incredibly supportive dad and sisters, Lisa and Gena; but I really struggled during the weekdays while I was away from home. Two weeks before my mom passed away, we had our final conversation and she told me that she was worried about how I would be after she was gone. I told her, "Mom, I'm going to be OK and I'm going to help other college students also coping with illness, in your honor. It's going to be called AMF." She responded by saying "unconditional love" and giving the best smile in the world. She passed away two weeks later on October 26, 2004. We held her memorial service a few days after her death, and I returned to school the following week.

When I returned to campus, I channeled all of my sadness, anger, and other grief reactions toward my mission to create something that would honor my mom and help others like me. I started by reaching out to faculty and staff from the counseling center, deans' offices, and campus ministry to find out what was available and to enlist their support. I made announcements in classes that "I just lost my mom, and I want to connect with others for support." Soon, dozens of students began seeking me out to share their stories. I realized that a large number of students were dealing with illness and grief on my campus, but no one was talking about it, so everyone felt alone. We could empathize with one another's challenges, like how college is supposed to be "carefree," how hard it was to relate to peers who made huge deals out of relatively small issues compared to what we were going through, and how classmates can be completely insensitive when they learn about one's grief. It was clear that a program like this was needed to connect us and give us a voice.

I began by creating a student organization called Students of AMF at Georgetown for grieving students that included a peer-led grief support group as well as a community service group so that grieving students and their peers could channel their energy toward volunteering in honor of deceased loved ones. AMF was a dual acronym for "Ailing Mothers and Fathers" and my mother's name, "Anne Marie Fajgenbaum." Each struggling student who shared his or her story of loneliness and limited peer support motivated me to work harder to improve and spread AMF. Every time I was sad about my mother's passing, I channeled more energy into honoring her life through this program. When I was frustrated about the fact that cancer had taken my mom, I focused harder on studying my pre-med materials and organizing more events to raise money for cancer research. What began as a group of five bereaved students meeting in a common room grew to include more than 400 members of the Georgetown community. Soon, students from other campuses around the U.S. wanted to start similar groups. I found research indicating that this was not just a Georgetown issue: 35–48 percent of college students have grieved the death of a loved one within the last two years (Balk, Walker, and Baker, 2010).

In 2006, I worked with my best friend, Ben Chesson, to co-found National Students of AMF, a nonprofit support network for college students grieving the illness or death of a loved one. We achieve our ongoing mission by creating Campus Chapters that include a peer-led grief support group and a community service group, offering online resources, and raising national awareness about young adult grief. We recently changed our name to just AMF, which now stands for "Actively Moving Forward," and we support grieving college students and young adults. I feel so fortunate to receive emails weekly from students in AMF chapters that say things like "I don't know what I would have done without AMF," "AMF helped me to stay in school." Of course, I think of my mom, the original AMF.

I am now an Adjunct Assistant Professor of Medicine in Hematology/Oncology at the University of Pennsylvania, where I focus on advancing cancer, Castleman disease, and other rare diseases through global collaboration. I am no longer the Board Chair for AMF. Co-founder, Ben Chesson, has taken on that important role, and I am still a member of the AMF Board of Directors. While AMF has reached students on more than 200 college campuses in the U.S., and it continues to make a deep impact in the lives of students on campuses with active chapters, I lose sleep at night thinking about the thousands of grieving students who don't have an AMF chapter on their campus and are in need of support and connection with others. This is why I decided to co-author this book with Heather.

I also wanted to share four lessons that I've learned through my personal grieving process. First, helping others through support and community service has been very therapeutic for me, and I've heard this from many of our AMF members. The community service component is a particularly helpful way to get guys, like myself, to confront some of their emotions—through actively doing something. Along the same lines, I also get tremendous therapeutic benefit from dedicating my life to fighting cancer. Second, the power of peer support and being able to speak with others who "get it" cannot be underestimated; my support group at Georgetown was my lifeline. Third, we all express our emotions differently, so it is essential that we encourage people struggling with grief to express their emotions in whatever way is most helpful for them. Fourth, even though it has been over ten years, I still miss my mom and wish that she were still here. But the sadness and intensity has certainly decreased over the years, so that I'm able to integrate my memories and the lessons she taught me to be able to actively move forward.

As authors, we have organized the narratives included in this book based on primary themes. We each independently read all of the narratives multiple times, took notes during those readings, met to discuss our notes, and finally determined our joint understanding of the key themes in the stories. Then we selected the two to four narratives that best highlight each theme. Each chapter begins with a description of a theme followed by the narratives that particularly highlight that theme. Each chapter ends with a few questions for reflection. We encourage you to keep a companion notebook with you as you read through the book to write down notes and your answers to the chapter questions for reflection at the end of each chapter.

The 12 themes do not capture all aspects of the narratives but do provide readers with a starting point or thread for their reading of the stories. The themes are overlapping in their focus and likely interact with one another. Do keep in mind that some of the themes (e.g., sense of isolation) are present in virtually all of the stories whereas others (e.g., forced maturity) are more prominent in certain stories and less so in others. The final two chapters offer tips for grieving college students and young adults and also tips for those who are in a position to support grieving students (e.g., family, friends, counselors, support group facilitators, faculty, staff, and administrators in higher education). In order to further enhance the usefulness of the book, we have also provided author background information for the stories based on factors such as who died (e.g., parent, sibling), cause of death (e.g., illness, accident), and experience of death prior, during, or after college (see the Appendix).

A point to consider in terms of the generalization of the themes is that the individuals who provided narratives for this book are a specific group of grieving college students. They were all at some point connected with National Students of AMF in the U.S., and the majority are white and female and were recently graduated alumni who attended college at the traditional age (i.e., 18–25). Of note, we intentionally removed all comments about National Students of AMF that were not crucial to the author's narrative or to the specific theme. We did not want to offer repeated description of the role of peer-led grief support and community service, when most college students and young adults do not have access to such a program.

Overall, we want to thank each and every one of the young adults who contributed to this book. We hope that their narratives speak to you as much as they did to us.

CHAPTER 1

Feeling Alone

A sense of feeling alone is an experience expressed by grievers of all ages but perhaps even more so by college students and young adults. Nearly all of the 33 authors described a distance, lack of connection, and feeling of separation and isolation from their non-grieving peers and often from family members as well. They had difficulty easily identifying peers who had experienced grief. Their sense of isolation was complex and sometimes paradoxical. They described a sense of loneliness and a need to pretend everything was OK even though they actually struggled to find a place where they *were* completely alone (e.g., always a roommate or classmate somewhere nearby) to genuinely and freely express their grief.

The authors reported an internal struggle over whether or not to talk about their grief with their peers. On the one hand, they described a desire to express their grief to others, to not have to pretend that everything was OK. On the other hand, they were concerned that sharing about their grief would burden others and "bring others down." In addition, they did not have confidence that their non-grieving peers would be capable of offering the support that they needed (e.g., listening in a nonjudgmental way, recognizing depth and extent of grief). In some cases, the authors had had past negative experiences with trying to talk with their peers about their grief and in other cases it was not clear whether grieving students' fears were based on experience or were more connected with untested negative expectations. The authors described frustration related to their peers' apparent avoidance of topics likely related to their grief (e.g., no longer talking about their own mothers). This avoidance was interpreted by our authors as meaning that their peers didn't *want* to talk about the death; a few authors acknowledged that their peers may have been avoiding the topic in an attempt to be supportive (e.g., thinking that avoiding topics would prevent pain for the grieving peer). The authors expressed confusion regarding not knowing who would understand and who would care enough to listen.

Our authors described a paradox of feeling lonely, because they were surrounded by others who did not understand what they were experiencing, but at the same time they were also seeking solitude and a way to escape. As many of the authors worked to pretend that everything was fine, they struggled internally with the desire to be alone, to be themselves in their grief. The college environment presented no opportunities for solitude in which they could let down their guard, release thoughts and feelings, and reconnect with their loved one. Students described feeling particularly lonely on special days such as move-in day, parents day, holidays/anniversaries.

This sense of aloneness is further paradoxical, because research indicates that approximately 40 percent of college students have experienced the death of someone they cared about within the previous two years (Balk *et al.*, 2010). We expect this number increases further for recently graduated young adults. Thus, a large percentage of young adults have experienced deaths and are actually not alone (in fact, there may be another person just down the hall), but everyone feels alone because no one talks about their death experiences. Western society generally prefers to avoid discussions of death and grief (Straker, 2013). Interestingly, our authors occasionally acknowledged a "cycle of silence" on college campuses. A few described situations where they did not know that a friend had experienced the death of a loved one until encountering the friend at a grief support group meeting. Both were grieving in isolation, struggling side by side, but alone in their silence.

Part of the sense of aloneness was also related to their new community (i.e., college environment) being unable to help with keeping the memory of their loved one alive. In their hometown, they had people who knew their loved one, who understood the essence of the person, and who could share memories with them. At college, the burden was on them to try and communicate the importance of their loved one's presence and now absence from their life, a burden that could prove too difficult and painful to approach.

A few authors (not in this chapter) reported using Facebook as a place to share their grief or remember a loved one, but they often did not receive the reactions that they had hoped for. It, unfortunately, did not help them to feel less alone. Though Facebook "connects" you with thousands of "friends" and "people you may know," it seems to have a limited role for connecting grievers and helping them to feel less alone.

Though most of the authors focus on their experiences with grief during the college years, we recognize that young adult grievers newly graduated from college share many common challenges. In fact, leaving college and the college environment, despite it not always being the most supportive, can leave young alumni feeling even more isolated than before.

We have included the following three stories that we believe demonstrate the sense of aloneness that grieving college students and young adults can experience.

Tiffany

Sex: Female

Age: 28

Time since death loss:
11 years, 2 months

Prior to college

Death loss: Father

Aneurysm

In high school, my younger sister Vickie and I played varsity volleyball together. Our parents came to every game, and each weekend we had all-day tournaments. October 20, 2001 began like all the others—we got up at 6am on Saturday and ate breakfast in the car, while our parents drove to some local high school for the tournament. Two things made this tournament different though: (1) I was being presented on the seniors' homecoming court that night at the football game, and (2) it was the last time I ever spoke to my dad.

My dad had suffered a minor heart attack a month earlier. Nothing major; his cardiologist just prescribed some blood thinners, better diet, more exercise. We counted ourselves lucky. When he felt a little weird, his doctor ordered some blood tests. They came out "safe"—just a cold, get some rest. But while watching us play the next day, my dad complained about an insane headache and spent most of the tournament slouched over in his chair feeling very ill. He was determined to watch every second we were on the court, and stayed through the last set Vickie was playing.

I was so excited about being on homecoming court that I left early to go home and get ready. I barely got out a "Love you Dad, see you later," as I kissed him and rushed out the door. My sister stayed for another match before also going home to get ready. My dad was feeling too ill to drive by the end of the tournament, so our teammate's parents took him back to our house. My mom put him straight to bed. I had already left for the game and dance.

The presentation of homecoming court was amazing. I had the best time in my gown and wearing a tiara, the whole shebang. The dance was even better, and we were having the time of our lives.

And then I got a call from my aunt—we had to go to the hospital right away. "Your dad is not OK. Leave the dance now." I thought, *oh no, he had another heart attack.* My best friend Brian drove me and Vickie straight to the ER, and he left me there with a hug and his jacket, since I didn't have anything else on me to keep me warm. My sister and I walked in to find our entire family in the waiting room, crying in a circle around a doctor. I was so confused. The doctor was talking, but I only heard bits and pieces. "It's very bad…4 percent chance of survival." *Did he just say 4 percent…4 percent?! That's low. Wait, this is MY dad you are talking about?* "…aneurism… emergency brain surgery…vegetable…death." *Wait, what? No, this can't be happening…I don't understand.*

Someone, an aunt maybe, hugged me and my sister very close from behind and wouldn't let go, as if she knew something was going to forever change our lives in ways we could not grasp in that moment. My thoughts swirled as tears streamed out of my eyes. They felt so foreign, like someone else was crying. I was so lost trying to understand the words that had just slapped me in the face. *Four percent? Really? There's no way. That's too low to be a real number.*

My mom looked so scared. She kept worriedly glancing over at me and Vickie. Everyone did. *What did they know that I didn't? Didn't the doctor say he was going to do the surgery, and then everything has to be OK. It has to be…*

Life doesn't always work out like that. They had overdosed my dad's blood-thinners. His veins and capillaries were bursting in his brain. My mom discussed many things with the doctor and with the other adults, always looking back at me and Vickie. She decided that we were going for the long shot, our "Hail Mary" emergency brain surgery. She knew deep down that it was too late, but she did not want me and Vickie to go through the rest of our lives with the guilt of *What if?* I'm very thankful to her for that decision. So they scheduled the surgery. Hours blended into days, and it didn't occur to us that we were still in our homecoming outfits two days later until an aunt brought us more comfortable clothes. At some point the surgeon came out, nervously clutching his hands. They had done the best they could to stop the bleeding and fix what damage had been done. It was just too late. He asked my mom in a low voice about "pulling the plug" and organ donation.

And just like that, my family went from four to three, and I found myself without adequate words when it came time to say goodbye. I watched as if it was a sad movie or something—someone else's life. I watched many faces of disbelief and sorrow come to say goodbye. I watched my usually unexpressive grandfather become teary as he bent over to kiss his oldest son goodbye on his forehead. And I watched my mom hold me and my sister with one arm and my dad's hand with the other, choke out a "Goodbye sweetheart, love you always," and turn to leave the room, never looking back.

And then it was my turn. A kiss on the cheek, which was still warm, and a simple "Love you, Dada." The same thing I said when we passed each other on the stairs every day before school. That's it. That was my goodbye. The next time I saw my dad was at his funeral. It sort of looked like him in the casket, but the coldness and sadness coming from that body certainly was not the same silly, dorky, amazing man who had been my father just a few weeks before. *Who would be there for our family picture when I graduated in June? Who would walk me down the aisle at my wedding? Who would be the grandfather of my kids?* These fears haunted my thoughts from that moment on and still creep up when I think about these important life moments, moments my dad won't be there.

A few weeks later, I was interviewing for college. I teared up when they asked about my parents and just left the room. For months, all I wanted to do was hide from everyone and everything. There were countless nights when I would come home feeling so unsafe and cry myself to sleep. I walked around the halls of my high school feeling like everyone was staring at me, feeling like they knew my deep, dark, sad secret that wasn't a secret at all, but also sensing that no one wanted to or knew how to talk about him or my grief. It was this giant elephant in the room, bursting out of me at every moment—*my dad DIED! He died, he's gone. I feel so much pain, and nothing at all.* But no one heard me screaming silently. No one saw how much I just needed someone to care, to hear my story, to listen about my dad. And because this subconscious, mourning, pained person was crying out inside of me 100 percent of the time while never actually uttering a single word, my existence felt heavier.

Time basically stood still for me, while the weeks and months passed. And on an ordinary, gray day in January, my mom, my sister, and I drove up to Sunset Beach in San Francisco, CA, where my parents had had their first date over 30 years ago, and scattered my dad's ashes. In February, when deciding where to go to college, I knew I had to stay close to home. Despite always having dreamed of the Ivy Leagues, I felt like I couldn't go far—I needed to be near my family, people who knew what my life had been like before, who understood the nuances of all that had happened in the last year. So, in the fall of 2002, almost one year since the day my dad died, I started college at UCLA.

The start of college was exciting, scary, fun, and awful, all at the same time. It was a rush of new faces, experiences, and freedoms. But as my new friendships became deeper and I needed to talk about my loss, I realized that I didn't know how to share the most defining moment in my life with those who were becoming my best friends. I didn't want to make anyone feel awkward or sad. I didn't know how to introduce everyone to this major part of me—the part of me that isn't always smiling and cries during cheesy dad moments in movies; the part of me that will forever gasp and feel a faint ache in my heart during father–daughter dances at weddings; the part of me that is deathly afraid of forgetting. I wanted so desperately to tell them about that side of me, but I didn't have the words.

It got to the point where most conversations were an internal struggle for me about whether to bring it up and risk being a downer or treated differently, or to just keep seeming normal, happy, and untroubled. I usually opted for the "safe" route, and felt more alone than ever. Being in a triple room also doesn't lend itself to silently crying yourself to sleep, so I would run away to empty corners of the campus just to cry. And when that didn't help anymore, I would jump in my car and drive the two hours from LA to San Diego, to go sit on the edge of a cliff with a 180-degree view of the ocean in front of me. I would sit there for hours, and just cry. Big, deep sobs. I would cry so hard and so long, and then I'd pick myself up and drive two hours back home like nothing had happened. I would go eat dorm dinner with my floor mates, always suffering from "allergies" to explain my poofy eyes. I felt like no one could understand or make it feel less awful, and I had no idea how to cope.

The first time I went back home after moving to college was for my dad's first death anniversary. I was stunned that an entire year had passed. I sat at his desk, which was still unchanged, and began to write out every single memory I could possibly remember about him. *Every single one!* Pages and pages and pages of scraps of stories, smudged with my tears as I wrote. I was so scared that the years would roll by as fast as this last one had, and that I would forget. That I would forget how he would make everyone laugh, or forget what it was like to dance around to Backstreet Boys with him to embarrass my sister, or just forget who he was completely. I still fear that sometimes.

I wanted to preserve everything just as it had been when he was alive, to see his same books arranged the same way, to stay in the same house forever—a desperate attempt to keep some normalcy in my life. But life moves on—the bookcase broke and the books tumbled into a mess. My mom sold the house a few years later; she even remarried. I'm thankful now, because these things forced me to let go and move on, away from the anger and sadness. Over the years, we've all forgotten a lot of things, and sometimes find ourselves looking for validation from each other—"Remember that one time when Dad…"—only to realize that all the stories are at best a little fuzzy. And that's OK. Fuzzy details doesn't mean forgetting him or loving him less; it just means that we're healing.

With time, I also became more comfortable telling people the stories about my dad—who he was, how he died. My friends saw his pictures and sometimes asked about him…or if they didn't, I would make a point of telling them about him, of letting that inner me speak up and tell her story. In 2007, six years after my dad had passed away, I felt very at peace with my grieving and healing. Quite a few death anniversaries and birthdays of his had passed without me crying, and I could talk about him without getting choked up. I felt like that giant weight of the world, my big secret, was alleviated. And I thought I was getting to the point where I would cry less in dad moments in movies. I was wrong; I started law school, and on the seventh anniversary of my dad's death, it felt like I was right back in college. I was telling a friend the same story I had retold so often without crying, and it hit me like a ton of bricks—seven years is so close to ten. And ten is *such* a long time for him to be gone. Pretty soon, it would be 15, and then 17, and then he will have been gone longer than he was alive in my lifetime. *Would I forget him? Would I forget those little things that made him my dad?* I freaked out. I walked around Philly for an entire day, oblivious to the cold and the world, looking for flowers at the start of winter. Seven hours and many tears later, I finally found some beautiful subtle blue baby orchids to honor his memory and the day.

I realized then that the grieving process isn't a straight line. It's a big jumble, and some years are better than others. That had been a doozie of a year. And last year, on the seven-year anniversary of my friend's mom's passing, I asked my friend how things were. She said fine, good. I shared my story about my tormented seven-year anniversary, and she just burst out, "God it's so awful, you really felt like this too?" We both just started tearing up. In that moment, I remembered the times right after my dad died when teachers, friends, and strangers had shared with me their own personal stories of loss. While reaching out to help me grieve, they too were helping themselves. I was now on the other side of this cycle of grieving and giving and healing.

It's been 11 years now—a long, impossible journey. My world crumbled under my feet, and I've had to rebuild it anew, one brick at a time. Time does heal, but not every moment can be better than the last. The process of grief is necessarily up and down, and you never know how any single day will hit you. All you can do is roll with the punches and keep going. You find peace in your memories and in helping others get through their pains. You never fully outgrow experiences like these because they sear your soul. But you do adapt and live again, and find new joys in life.

Two of my favorite quotes sum up how I feel about the grieving process and healing: "The first ones to help you up are the ones who know how it feels to fall down," and: "Through my grieving process, I don't want to be admired for my strength nor pitied for my weakness. I just want to be understood. Some days I may be strong, some days I may be weak. I choose neither."

Ashley

Sex: Female

Age: 27

Time since death loss:
7 years, 4 months

During college

Death loss: Father

Cancer

October 11, 2004. "Your dad has cancer."

Just two weeks after watching my grandfather pass away from the very same disease, I heard the doctor say these words as if I was watching a bad dream montage in a movie. Only this was not a movie, it was my life. I was a sophomore at Georgetown University studying to be a nurse. In a blink of an eye my life had become a living example of the diseases we studied in class.

Being from a small town in Indiana with a population of 1400 and no stoplight, I often felt out of place at Georgetown. In a world of pastels and popped collars, I felt as though I had accidently stumbled into a J.Crew catalog. I was not surprised with my first reaction to the news about my dad—transferring to a college back home. The thought of going back to school, a place that already felt so foreign, was less than appealing.

My dad on the other hand, a hopeless academic, would not hear of it. He insisted that he would be fine and that I needed to return to Georgetown to continue my education. So back to school I went.

Eight months later on a warm summer night, in the quiet of our home surrounded by family and friends, he peacefully passed away.

That fall I made the journey back to school and grieved in the quiet of my dorm room.

Once back at school I often felt alone. My roommates and friends were focused on schoolwork, parties, and their latest crush. I, on the other hand, was worrying about my family that I left back home to grieve.

One day, after forgetting the recipe for my dad's favorite chili, I began to cry while at the stove. My roommates happened to walk in and notice my tears. I quickly wiped them away and asked about their day. After a few days of strange stares and awkward encounters, I asked them about their behavior and they responded, "We just don't know how to act around you any more." I was baffled that my one tearful display of emotion had made them feel so uncomfortable.

At that point, I decided it was best to keep my emotions and grief to myself. I found my own ways of coping. I grieved by putting a smile on my face and insisting that I was fine—only I wasn't.

Before my dad became sick, religion played an important role in my life and after he passed away I often found respite from grief in church. My strong belief that if you were a good person your prayers would be heard was shaken with my dad's passing. Once back at school, I continued to go to church. I returned, slightly bitter and angry at God, but I returned. Through the friendship of a Jesuit priest at school who took me under his wing, I realized that my anger with God was not all bad. He explained that people do not waste time being angry at someone they do not love. So my anger with God was acceptable, he attested, because anger always trumps indifference.

Another way in which I coped was through running. At times I would bury my grief and emotion so deep that the only way to reach it was to run in the trails around Georgetown until finally my emotion would boil to the surface. I spent many days running alone in those woods, where it was safe to shed a tear without making others uncomfortable or worse, inviting them into the pain I was experiencing.

Months into my attempt to handle my grief alone I was convinced to visit a school counselor. I was very hesitant at first but in the end it was one of the best decisions I ever made. I began the first session stating, "Please don't ever ask me how something makes me feel." He laughed, as he often did at me, and that is exactly what I needed. One day he asked me why I had such a difficult time talking to my friends about my dad. I responded simply, stating, "I don't want to make other people sad." Once again he laughed and stated, "Well, you need to get over that." After a year of seeing him weekly, it was time for our sessions to end. Before we finished he told me something I will never forget. A few weeks before our first session he too had lost his father to cancer. He told me that through the process of working with me and hearing my stories he had started to heal. It was the first time I realized that by sharing my stories and feelings I could help others.

I was lucky to be in the class of 2007 at Georgetown University and that luck would show itself when I needed it the most. In the midst of a particularly isolating time I met a fellow classmate who had just tragically lost his mother to cancer mere weeks before my dad passed. He told me about a support group he was starting for students who had a sick or deceased parent. I was reluctant; the thought of sharing my story and feelings with a bunch of strangers terrified me.

I went, I listened, I shared and for the first time I felt like I wasn't alone. Being in a room full of people with sick or deceased parents sounds depressing, but it wasn't. It was a group of instant friends. We did races to support causes close to each of us and we had buddy systems to call each other on particularly difficult days. More importantly, we started to heal.

I still remember the first time I laughed after my dad passed away. I mean really laughed without feeling guilty that I had not observed the proper length of grieving and suffering. I was at a bus stop with a new friend who didn't know me before my dad passed; he didn't know the happy-go-lucky innocent me untainted by death and grief. He just knew me. In an unassuming moment that snuck up on me I laughed, unabashedly. It was the first time in months that I had let go and laughed. A moment that passed without him noticing made me feel like a part of me was back, and it was spectacular.

When you lose a parent at a young age you are forced to grow up much faster than any person should. I often looked at my classmates with envy; I was jealous of their innocence. It was a lonely time and having a safe place and a supportive group of people who understood me was the greatest blessing. I am forever thankful that I had that outlet.

Even seven years later as I write this in a café where I have started my new life, tears quietly fall down my cheek as I remember, with awe, what I was faced with at the all-too-young age of 20. I only hope that others faced with similar trials and tribulations have an outlet and find comfort in my story knowing that they are not alone.

Michelle

Sex: Female

Age: 26

Time since death loss: 8 years and 12 years

Prior to college

Death loss: Brother and father

Suicide/schizophrenia (brother), mesothelioma (father)

I grew up in the suburbs of New York City, in a place where families did not lock their doors or worry about many of the issues that plague the majority of the world. However, a month before my freshman year of high school, the protective sheath around my family was suddenly broken. While away at summer camp, my 27-year-old brother Tom took his own life. As I tried to make sense of what had happened, previously unfamiliar terms like "suicide" and "schizophrenia" became central words in my vocabulary. I had an immense amount of questions and hardly any answers. *What was this "schizophrenia" and why did my brother have it? Could I catch it somehow? Why did he selfishly take his own life and leave us behind to miss him?*

The most confusing aspect of his death was the multitude of emotions I felt. I expected to be sad, yet I was not prepared for the anger, guilt, and shame that accompanied the grief. Most peers in my town had not experienced the death of a significant family member—let alone one that was sudden and traumatic—so I felt as though everyone was talking about my family. I imagined they were whispering, "Aren't those the girls whose brother committed suicide?" as my sister and I walked down the halls. I felt trapped between wanting to crawl into a hole and hide from the world, and wanting to connect with my friends and feel supported by them.

Four years later—during my senior year of high school—I was hit by another big blow. Almost two years after his initial diagnosis, my dad died at age 63 from mesothelioma, a rare and fatal cancer of the lung lining. I thought things like, *Why me? This isn't fair! I don't want to feel this way anymore! Will this sadness ever end?*

Instead of enjoying the events typically celebrated at the end of high school (e.g., prom, graduation), I found myself just trying to survive them by putting on a brave face. I didn't want anyone else to know how much I was hurting. As a result, I did a lot of my grieving in private. I would cry myself to sleep for hours, inevitably having to turn the pillow over to the dry side because the side I was lying on was drenched in tears.

Although not my first experience with loss, the death of my dad had a profound impact on my time at college. My world had collapsed and all I wished was for him to magically return somehow. There were times I thought I saw his face in a crowd of people, only to be disappointed when my quickening steps brought me face-to-face with a stranger. I felt tricked on these occasions. A part of me knew I wouldn't see his face in person again, but a part of me held on to hope that a miracle had happened and it would be him.

As a new student in a new place, I struggled with how to present myself to the outside world. Questions like "Where do your parents live?" or "What does your dad do for a living?" made me freeze momentarily; I would quickly try to assess if I wanted to reveal my loss to the person asking. *How will this person react to me telling them? Is it worth me having to explain? Maybe I should just lie.* On occasion, I *did* lie. "My dad works in computer software design," "We're very close," or, "Yup, I can't wait to see them on Parents Weekend!" It seemed like no one else had lost a parent so this was the easier response.

I also found that I had very few places on campus where I could express my grief. Gone were the nights with my tear-drenched pillow, as I had a roommate just three feet away who would witness my every tear and hear my every sob. I began to relish my time in the shower, where the showerhead's stream washed away my tears before anyone could see them. I felt at peace there, with my self and with my grief. Another beloved place was a quiet spot right outside the university's gym. The hill overlooked the river and at night reflected the lights of the buildings. This place became my oasis, where I would sit night after night, listening to music, and thinking about my dad.

As I began settling into my new life at college, I discovered that my grief was still very raw and fresh. I connected with a therapist at the free counseling service on campus, but peer support was still lacking. My new friends tried to be supportive and sympathetic, yet I found myself withdrawing from them as well; they just "didn't understand" what I was feeling. I was afraid that I would be burdening them with my grief, so I didn't reach out when I needed to. They were afraid they would make me upset by asking how I was doing, so they never asked. This created a "cycle of silence" that perpetuated isolation in my loss.

I also began to feel distanced from my mom and sister who were still up in New York; my sense was that they were deepening their relationship with one another and that I was the odd one out. Feeling hurt and alone, I yearned for home, my family, and my friends from high school, who not only knew me inside and out, but also knew my dad and what kind of person he was. I had the distinct notion that the life I had previously known was drifting farther away from my grasp, and all I wanted to do was rewind the clock to the time when my dad was alive. *How could all these changes have happened so fast?*

Another adjustment was trying to meet the demands of a college workload and keep my grades up, while battling some of the physical manifestations of grief: exhaustion, lack of concentration, decreased motivation, etc. Previously a straight-A student in high school, I now found myself struggling to get assignments in on time and to get through the readings. Lower grades resulted in poorer self-esteem and a basic questioning of how I could function in the world without my dad; I felt lost.

A few months into my time on campus, I heard about a new support group for grieving students. I nervously attended a group, not sure of how I would be able to relate to the other students. We talked about issues such as getting through the holidays, how to communicate needs to friends, and how to cope with our feelings. I felt like I fit in perfectly. One of the biggest surprises on that first night was seeing one of my friends in the group. She had lost her mother when she was 12 and was still grieving her absence. I was amazed by the idea that someone in my social circle had lost a parent too. *How did I not know this about her?* I realized that the "cycle of silence" was the reason why this major topic in our lives never came up. She ended up becoming one of my closest friends and a true model for how to be resilient in the face of significant loss.

Slowly, but surely, I learned to manage my grief and was able to talk more openly about my experiences with death. Knowing that others were going through the same thing (when I was feeling very alone in my loss experience) was such a relief. I felt that the group members understood me implicitly; there was no need to explain or apologize for the feelings I was having. I found a community of people who understood that the grief process would lessen in intensity over time, but ultimately would be a lifelong process. We would always miss our loved ones and the group was a place for those feelings. Even though the grief process was very often painful and scary, knowing that I had a network of grieving peers to turn to made me feel that my support group family would cushion even "rock bottom." This gave me hope and ultimately was one of the major factors in helping me heal my broken heart.

Today, seven years out of college, I have a Master's degree in Mental Health Counseling and a Certificate in Thanatology (i.e., study of death and dying). I work as a bereavement counselor for a hospice, providing counseling for family members whose loved ones have died on our hospice program. It is such a privilege to be there with others during their times of grief, walking with them hand-in-hand through the darkness. This is what I feel I was *meant* to do. My losses certainly changed my life, but changed it for the good by giving me purpose and a sense of direction. I know that I would not be where I am professionally without having had to do a lot of personal work around my grief, and I am forever indebted to the students in my support group and my therapists for being guiding lights. Thank you for understanding that grief is not something that just goes away.

Questions for Reflection

Please reflect on and/or write out answers to the following questions:

1. Think about a time when you felt alone in your grief? What do you believe kept you from reaching out to friends, family members, or other supporters?

2. Think about a time that you felt connected with another in your grief. What connected you with that person?

3. If you could go back to a time when you felt alone in your grief, what would you like to have done differently to identify friends, family members, or other supporters who you could have turned to for support? If you are currently grieving, what are some of the things that you can do now to identify and connect with others who get it?

For supporters:

What might you say and do to encourage the grieving college students and young adults in your life to turn to you for support with their grief now and in the future?

CHAPTER 2

Continuing Connection, Memorialization, and Active Grief and Coping

The concept that the intensity of grief after someone dies is often proportional to the love for the deceased person when he or she was alive helps to explain why grievers often wish to maintain connections with loved ones (Klass, Silverman, and Nickman, 1996). Grief is a reflection of love. Not surprisingly, the authors described a strong desire to maintain a connection with their loved one who died, to not forget them and to keep their memory alive through their thoughts and/or actions. This desire was often expressed through individual and private actions such as writing to or talking out loud to the loved one, writing all they could remember about their loved one, and recognizing symbols of the loved one such as things he or she loved (e.g., water, crossword puzzles, rugby).

The authors also described keeping their loved one's essence alive by exerting particular qualities (similar to their loved one's qualities) in their lives, talking with others who knew their loved one well, or sharing stories with others who never had a chance to meet him or her. Objects (e.g., jewelry, clothing) were also sometimes important in keeping their loved one's memory close at hand. Another form of memorialization involved the honoring of their loved one's life and death through their choice of occupation and/or purpose in life. The authors often reported remaining connected to their loved one through living in a way that he or she would be proud of.

In addition, many students expressed the desire to memorialize (i.e., preserve the memory of, commemorate) their loved one through what we have termed "altruistic instrumental grieving" (i.e., taking actions that directly benefit and offer service to others—often others who are also grieving—to "honor" a deceased loved one). The authors described volunteering for service organizations that made tangible and real contributions to the world. There was a sense of perhaps reconnecting with an ability to add to the world and gaining a feeling of control in the midst of so much confusion, sense of loss, and the lack of control that comes with death. These grievers reported direct benefit from these altruistic acts, because helping others in memory of a loved one enabled that loved one's life to continue and also seemed to give meaning to their death (i.e., their death spurred good deeds for others).

Scholars in the bereavement field have referred to the concept of active grieving as instrumental grieving (Doka and Martin, 2010) because these grievers express, experience, and adapt to grief by using instruments or activities, such as exercise, to cope. On the other hand, intuitive grievers often experience grief as waves of feelings that they strongly express, for example, through crying or talking. These grievers are best supported through support groups, counseling, and other opportunities that allow for the expression of feelings. Gender, culture, and personality complexly interact in the development of a primary pattern of grief, men can be more instrumental in their grief and women can be more intuitive. However, there is no right way to grieve, and many individuals display both types of pattern at different times. We highlight this information to make the point that not everyone is going to benefit from a particular coping strategy. It is important to consider many outlets and determine which is most helpful for you.

I (David) created AMF along with my best friend in memory of my mother, and the organization shares many common traits with her, such as compassion, empathy, and supportiveness. Her giving spirit gets to continue beyond her death through AMF. Creating this organization and observing the impact that AMF is having has been extremely therapeutic for me. I have also personally benefited from leading fundraising events for cancer research in memory of my mom, because I feel less helpless and more connected with my mom by battling a common enemy. This process is also something that we have heard about frequently from other grieving young adults.

Memorializing a loved one does not have to be through establishing an organization. As you will read in the narratives, memorialization can take place through doing an activity your loved one enjoyed doing or through keeping an important object close to you.

The authors also described active expressions of their grief that did not appear to be directly linked to their loved one who died, but served as outlets for their energy connected with their loss. These active expressions ranged widely from horseback riding, running, and playing sports to painting, drawing, and baking bread. At times these approaches seemed to be ways to take a break from their grief and at others times the authors acknowledged that they were ways to actively move forward through their grief. Both purposes are worthy and important.

We have included the following four stories that we believe demonstrate how continuing connection, memorialization, and active grief and coping can present for grieving college students and young adults.

Kristen S.

Sex: Female

Age: 23

Time since death loss:
6 years, 6 months

Prior to college

Death loss: Mother

Suicide/bipolar disorder

My mom, Rita, was the kind of person you don't meet every day. She had a bright smile and an infectious laugh that could make even the darkest of days brighter. She had an incredible mind and excelled at any endeavor she undertook. She had the biggest heart of anyone I've ever known and her generosity was unmatched. My mom also had bipolar disorder. Her illness was a part of her, but she did not let it define who she was as a person. First and foremost, she was a mother, a wife, a sister, an aunt, a teacher, and a friend.

My mom was diagnosed with bipolar disorder when I was eight years old. At the time, I really didn't understand what mental illness was. People kept telling me that my mom was "sick," but in my youthful innocence, I figured that since she didn't look sick, she must not be. My mom's illness took hold of her and for the next year her life was tumultuous. She separated from my father, started spending excessive amounts of money, and was acting erratically. My brother and I were caught in the middle of the chaos, and being young, we really didn't understand what was happening. After nearly a year of pain and anguish, my mother came up with a plan to kill herself. However, before she actually followed through, she reached out to her family who took her to hospital, where she was admitted to the inpatient psychiatric unit for several weeks. After weeks as an inpatient, and several months as an outpatient, my mom started to get better. She made amends with her family, reconciled with my father, and moved back home. For the next eight years, my life largely returned to normal. My family was together; we were healthy and we were happy.

About a month before my 16th birthday, my mom asked my dad to leave the house; she wanted a divorce. My dad sat my brother and me down and warned us that our mom was getting sick again. He mentioned some behaviors that were out of the ordinary, and told us that we needed to "watch her carefully." At the time, I hadn't noticed anything different, she seemed to be the same mom that I knew and loved.

On my 16th birthday, my mom broke down in a restaurant where I was celebrating with several friends. At that moment, I realized that my mom truly was sick. I was confused, sad, and worried about the future.

For the next year, my family life was chaos: court dates, restraining orders, threatening phone calls, screaming matches, and countless tears. In early May, my mom called me and told me that she was checking herself into the local psychiatric hospital, because she hadn't been sleeping and recognized that she was having a rough time. I remember visiting my mom in the hospital. I hated knowing that we only had a limited amount of time together and I was uncomfortable being watched constantly by the staff. But I was happy she was getting help and I was relieved because I felt like everything would be OK. When it was time to go, I gave my mom a hug and told her I loved her. I walked out, looking back to see her watching me with tears in her eyes.

She was released from the hospital on May 14, which happened to be Mother's Day. I couldn't go visit her at her apartment though because I was sick with a fever and a cough. I got caught up in my school life and still didn't go visit her, but spoke frequently with her on the phone. On the morning of May 18, I called my mom on my way to school. She sounded a little more down than usual, but she just said that she was tired from not sleeping well. I believed her and continued on talking about my plans for prom that weekend. That was the last time I would ever speak to my mom. No one could get in touch with her for the rest of the day and sometime in the middle of the night we reported her missing to the police. What followed was one of the most emotionally trying weekends of my young life. I was terrified about not being able to get in touch with her, but tried to remain hopeful that she was OK.

On May 22, her body was found. She had drowned herself in a lake on the golf course in the neighborhood I grew up in. I was devastated. I remember the look on my father's face and, even before he told me, I knew she was gone. My dad and I went to tell my brother what had happened; I have never felt more helpless in my life. We hugged each other and sobbed for what felt like hours.

Immediately after my mom died, I was devastated. I didn't know how I would ever be able to go on. My mom was my best friend, and within an instant, she was gone. I felt physically sick. Minutes after I found out she had died, I curled up in a ball on the bathroom floor. I couldn't catch my breath. My world was caving in on me.

The week after my mom died was a flurry of activity; family and friends brought food, flowers were delivered, we planned her memorial service, and we tried to make sense of what had happened. I wrote my mom's obituary with the help of one of my favorite cousins. My brother and I helped plan her memorial service with the help of several of my aunts and we both spoke at her service, which we called "A Celebration of Life."

The next few months were a blur. Since my mom had died toward the end of the school year during my junior year of high school, I was given a lot of flexibility in when I returned to school. I sort of eased myself back into it, initially going to the classes that I felt most comfortable with. I spent that summer doing what I loved most: surfing and spending time on the beach. I tried to keep busy, but I also gave myself plenty of time to relax.

When school started back in the fall, I threw myself into my schoolwork. I was involved with just about every extracurricular activity that I could be: student council, Beta Club, National Honor Society, Science Olympiad, Quiz Bowl…I spent the majority of my time at school. School had been my sanctuary when my mom was sick, and it remained that way after she died. I kept myself busy so that I didn't have to think about my grief. One year after my mom's death, I graduated high school at the top of my class. I felt a pang of sadness as I walked across the stage, knowing how proud my mom would have been.

I started college as a freshman at UNC-Chapel Hill, and that was when the reality of my mom's death began to sink in. I went from a relatively small school where everyone knew about my loss, to a huge university where only my friends from home knew about my mom. I found myself having to tell people about my mom, a task that was incredibly challenging. How do you tactfully tell someone that your mom killed herself? I recognized that I needed to talk about my loss and I sought help from the campus counseling center. I worked for several months with a therapist and then joined a grief support group. Slowly but surely, I started to feel better.

After a chance meeting, I connected with another student who had also lost her mom. Her mom didn't die by suicide, but just knowing that we were both missing our moms made a world of difference. We stayed in a fast food restaurant for literally four hours. We talked about our moms, our lives since their deaths, our families…we talked about anything and everything. For the first time since my mom had died, I felt like someone "got it." I felt like I wasn't alone. Together, we started a chapter of National Students of AMF on UNC's campus. This is a group of college students who are coping with the illness or death of a loved one. We got together every other week to talk about our experiences. We talked about our lives without our loved ones: the birthdays, holidays, and anniversaries; the moments where you reach for your phone to call them and then realize they're no longer here; the moments where you feel completely alone. This group was invaluable to me, and I am forever grateful for the connections I made.

Around the same time I got involved with AMF, I also started volunteering at a bereavement camp for children, Comfort Zone Camp. I have volunteered over 20 weekends of my time to help children who are coping with the death of a loved one. On Saturday night at camp, everyone has the opportunity to write a note to their loved one and place it in the bonfire. Each time I write a note to my mom, place it in the fire, and watch as the ashes are carried into the night sky, I feel more connected: connected not only to my mom, but to the wonderful people I meet at camp. I go to camp to be a support for the kids, but I truly feel that I take away as much or more than they do.

In 2010, I had the opportunity to walk in the Out of the Darkness Overnight Walk in Boston. The Overnight is an 18-mile journey through the night to support suicide awareness and prevention. For the first time in my life, I was surrounded by over 1000 other suicide survivors; the feeling was truly indescribable. One year later, I had the chance to walk in the Overnight again, this time in New York City. I met another girl in her twenties who had also lost her mother to suicide as a teenager. The connection we had was immediate, and we spent the entire evening sharing our stories, our laughter, and our tears.

I am currently in the final year of my graduate program where I am pursuing my Master's in Social Work. My interest in social work largely stemmed from my experiences with my mom, both when she was sick and after her death. I am anxious to see where my career choice will lead me and I hope to be a support to families who have experienced loss.

When my mom died, I made the decision to be truthful about her cause of death. As hard as it has been, I have never lied about how my mom died. When people ask, and they quite often do, I tell them that my mom had a mental illness and that she died by suicide as a result of her disease. No matter how many times I have had to tell people, I still feel my face flush and heart race as I wait for their reaction. More often than not they respond sympathetically and frequently mention someone in their life who also died by suicide. I have realized that by being open with my story, others are more open with me.

I have also been fortunate to have the unconditional love and support of a very large extended family. My brother and I are closer than most siblings I've ever met. We look out for each other, and I know that he is always there for me. My aunt, my mom's sister, was hugely supportive. She would talk to me on the phone for hours as I cried and remembered my mom. She would comfort me when I was upset with my dad. She never tried to replace my mom, but she stepped in and did motherly things. My friends have also been wonderful, and have supported me along every step of my grief journey.

After my mom's death, my relationship with my dad changed. I had always felt closer to my mom, but when she passed away, I realized that he was the only parent I had left. He was dating a woman I didn't get along with, and spent a lot of his time with his friends. In the moments that I needed him the most, I felt very much alone. However, I now realize that he was grieving too; he was doing the best he could at the time. Our relationship has greatly improved over the years, as we have both learned to be more open and honest with each other.

Six-and-a-half years later, I still miss my mom. I always will. She was my best friend, and she was an irreplaceable part of my life. Rather than moving on and forgetting, I try to concentrate on moving forward and remembering. Remembering all the good memories I shared with my mom: the movie nights spent curled up on the couch, our family vacations, the way she used to rub my back when I was sick, and the way she made me feel when she wrapped me in her arms for what truly were the most wonderful hugs.

People often comment on how well I seem to be doing despite my mom's death. The truth is, it's not the manner in which my mom died that has gotten me to where I am today, but, rather, it is the extraordinary way in which she lived her life; a life filled with compassion, empathy, and unconditional love. These are qualities that I hold on to in my heart and they continue to guide me as I walk this long journey.

Carolyn

Sex: Female

Age: 24

Time since death loss:
3 years, 5 months

During college

Death loss: Sister

Sudden/unclear cause

My little sister, Lizzie, passed away in 2009. At the time, she was 18 and had just finished her first year of college. We were on summer vacation and I went away for the weekend for a friend's birthday party. She went to a friend from high school's house near home for a small party. In the past, Lizzie had said that she thought that she was allergic to beer, so she didn't drink very often. From what her friends have told me, she was drinking but seemed fine when she went to bed. At some point in the night she had a reaction and her friends found her. By the time the ambulance arrived and she got to the hospital, it was too late to save her.

I woke up the next morning and had had a text from Liz around 2am asking what I was up to. I texted her back and tried to call her the next morning, but she didn't pick up. When I got home, my mom told me what had happened.

We still don't know exactly what happened to Lizzie because her friends and the police said there was nothing out of the ordinary and the autopsy and medical reports were inconclusive. Although it would be nice to know, I know that it wouldn't bring her back. I really just miss my sister and wish she was here.

For the first months, I mostly just cried. My parents, Lizzie's friends, and our parish priest were some of the most helpful people during that time. I think the best way that they showed that they understood was being able to talk to me about Lizzie and not being afraid to listen. Lizzie and I have some amazing friends who were here for us both before and after she died. Many of them came to visit our family after she died and have done many things to keep her spirit alive, whether they send a text on her birthday or do something nice for others in her name. I know it has been especially difficult for Lizzie's friends, some of whom were with Lizzie when she died, but they have been some of the best comfort and inspiration for me. I don't think Lizzie's friends realize how nice it is for us to see them, and I'm so grateful that she has people who care about her and bring her spirit to others.

My cousin was also really helpful. She and my aunt and uncle came to visit right after Lizzie died, and she helped by putting together a collage of pictures for Lizzie's wake. She's a teacher and always seems to know the right thing to say, and you can't help but be happy when she's around. There were a lot of things that I wanted to do for Lizzie's services, but didn't have the strength to do them, so it was so nice to have my cousin and some of Lizzie's friends fill in the pieces.

My friends from high school stayed with me throughout the week before Lizzie's funeral, and others came to Lizzie's services or tried to get me out of the house throughout the summer. I know it was difficult for them to try to cheer me up, but I am so thankful that they did.

My friends from school who *knew* Lizzie and were at her services were more helpful than others. I found that it was easiest to be around people who knew Liz and could talk about her like she was still here. Lizzie was hilarious, she was a great swimmer, and she was an amazing sister and friend. Sometimes, I just want to talk about her without someone giving me an "Are you OK?" look. People who knew her, or at least know how much I love her, understand that. I understand that it would be impossible to understand what I went through without knowing Lizzie, so I appreciated everyone's love and tried to remember that they were doing their best regardless of whether they were helpful.

In September, I had to go back to school for my senior year, which was a difficult transition, but was a helpful distraction. It was nice to see friends. Many of them had come to Lizzie's funeral or sent thoughtful cards, so it was nice to know I was going back to school with friends who had been so loving and thoughtful. With that said, it was very difficult to constantly be around people who haven't been through anything like losing Lizzie. I tried to call my parents whenever I started feeling upset, or to go to church and talk to God, which was helpful.

When I went back to school, I had to remind myself to try not to expect a lot from people who didn't know Lizzie well and didn't know what I was going through. While it was a nice distraction to go back to school, it was hard to deal with missing Lizzie when a lot of my friends never talked to me about her death. I didn't feel comfortable expressing emotions in front of friends who didn't know Lizzie or didn't seem to understand loss, which was particularly difficult. With that said, if I was in their shoes, I would have probably felt equally uncomfortable. In general, I think that avoiding Lizzie's death showed a lack of understanding. I have a few friends who never really said anything to me in person, and it was hard to get past that, although I had to move on. In the end, some of those people have become great friends, and I'm happy I forgave their lack of understanding in the early months. Before I lost Lizzie, I would have thought that it would be best not to make someone upset by saying something. Now I appreciate the strength it takes to comfort someone and listen, and hope I would do that if one of my friends went through something similar. Also, it really bothers me when friends use the term "blacked out" or refer to "dying" from drinking too much. Although we have no idea how Lizzie died or the role that alcohol may have played in her death, I find it extremely inconsiderate when people say things that allude to dying from drinking in front of me. Most of my close friends have never said these things, but I have had a few times where a friend has told a story about someone throwing up from alcohol or calling an ambulance and I wish they wouldn't have said anything.

In the end, I understand that everyone has their strengths in life and some people just aren't built to deal with loss. I can't hold that against them. I have learned to just rely on and be thankful for the many friends who have been supportive and understanding.

I'm religious and believe that Lizzie is with God but, regardless, it has been difficult to learn how to live without her. I often wear her jewelry or clothes, or will write her a text. Sometimes if I hear something that I know she'd think was funny, I'll just look up to Heaven and laugh. Although I'm learning to live without her here, I find myself struggling with keeping her spirit alive and with me in my day-to-day life at the same time. She was very positive and full of life, and I try to take her spirit with me, but often struggle.

Allison

Sex: Female

Age: 24

Time since death loss:
11 years, 1 month

Prior to college

Death loss: Mother

Scleroderma

Growing up in a household where the words "oxycontin" and "prednisone" were used as commonly as "soccer practice" and "the Disney Channel," I learned what it was to manage an illness from an early age. My mother was diagnosed with scleroderma, an auto-immune disease, shortly after my parents were married. The illness is known for the "hardening of the skin" that occurs as a part of the disease, causing an almost plastic look to the facial features. However, I never noticed this as a child; my mom was just my mom. I never thought our family was different growing up, though I knew my mom was sick and was in and out of the hospital a lot more than my other friends' parents.

My mother was the kind of person who was always there to help others and she did not often accept help willingly. In fact, she would often call the ladies who sat with her during the day the "Gestapo police" because they would not allow her to get out of bed. But because of their persistence my mother was able to conserve her energy for the most important tasks, namely the time she spent with me. I believe part of the reason I was able to cope with my mother's illness so well as a child was because she made it easy for me. My mom would somehow make chronic illness and disease funny or a game. I remember she would sit me down when she would get an infected cut or bruise that was turning red and have me circle the area with an ink pen. She would tell me that if the redness went outside of the circle, we would have to call her doctor. And when she had a digit of her finger amputated from an infection, she turned the remaining "stump" of the finger into a comical character, with a teensy tiny voice because it was a teensy tiny finger. It took me a long time to recognize how much my mother did to protect me from the trauma and sadness of disease through her antics and selfless courage. Later on in my life, a large amount of guilt plagued me because of this. For several years, I blamed myself for not understanding how ill she was, for not doing more for her, or for treating her poorly when she was ill (though fighting with Mom was a pretty normal preteen thing to do). But at the time, I was pretty unaware of what my mother was going through.

There is was one night I remember. It was the night that I started to realize her illness was getting serious. It was the summer of 2001, and I was 13. My father was traveling for the weekend in the mountains, as he did more often during the last six months of my mom's life—to meditate and come to terms with her dying, I suppose. I was downstairs watching television, and my mother was upstairs in her bedroom. I had taken her some soup a few hours earlier, along with a Coca-Cola, her favorite beverage. As the latest show on television ended, I realized that she had not called down the stairs to me since I had taken her the meal. I went upstairs to see if she had finished her food so I could bring her tray back downstairs. When I went upstairs, I saw she had not touched her dinner or her Coke. Instead, she was shivering on the bed, half curled up in a blanket, mumbling in a fitful looking sleep. As it was summer, I found it strange when she had asked for the blanket earlier in the day, but she obviously had not been feeling well. I asked her if she wanted me to reheat her soup, but she did not hear me and so I went to rouse her. But as I reached for her arm, I felt that her skin was ice cold. My senses were immediately heightened and my heart started racing. I tried to shake her awake, but she only opened her eyes slightly and said something incoherent about a bedpan. Recognizing she was not her normal self, I called a family friend to tell her what was going on. Together, the family friend and I decided I should call an ambulance. And so I did.

The rest of the evening was a bit of a blur, but I know there had to be a dozen people in my mother's bedroom at some point. I think they needed several people to help get her to the ambulance. After they took my mother to the hospital, I called a friend to tell her what had happened, but from what I remember there was mostly silence on the other line. I switched schools in between my sixth and seventh grade years, just a year before this incident. The transition was difficult for me as I moved from a liberal, peace-love-and-harmony oriented Montessori school to an academically rigorous and socially difficult college prep school. I found that most of my friends had no idea how to respond to the stories I would tell them about my mom, a trend that continued after my mother died.

Once my father returned, he told me that my mom had a paralyzed lung, and was unable to get enough oxygen. My mom had an oxygen tank with her at all times after that. I learned later that my mom almost died that night, but rallied through it as she had done and continued to do many times.

I think I knew my mom was going to die. I even remember asking my father about it a few months before my mother passed away; more to say it out loud than to actually get a response. He told me she was dying, and the only thing I could think to say at that point was, "What are we going to do?" I was 13 at the time, so I was not thinking of the things that I occasionally struggle with now as a young adult, such as living decades of my life without her to share it with, or entering new phases of life and surmounting challenges without her guidance and support. No, when I originally asked that question I was thinking mostly of the trivial things, such as doing the laundry, driving to school events, and making sure I had dental and haircut appointments set up. I had no concept of how much would actually change when she was gone.

My mother died on November 25, 2001, three days after Thanksgiving. I am still learning all of the details about what she went through medically, but essentially her organs were shutting down, and a risky surgery did not go well. Immediately following her death, I didn't totally understand what was happening. I knew she had died, but the concept of "forever" didn't really hit me until much later in life. In my head, I found this to just be another challenge for us to overcome, and I enjoyed the attention I got from sticking through it; another thing for which I felt extreme guilt later on in life. But, in some ways, my mother had taught me to grieve this way; she had taken life one day at a time, with an optimistic, rational attitude. She focused on the next steps. I was surrounded by this method of coping until the day that she died. Until then, my dad more often than not deferred to my mom on how to handle her illness and how to talk to me about it.

After she died, I was introduced to my dad's form of grieving, and it came with a lot of tears. My dad is a sensitive man, and though both of my parents worked as child and family psychologists, my father is much more of a feeler. Following my mom's death, my father entered a dark and shadowy phase. We moved out of my childhood home a month after my mother died, and it was torn down. Dad and I moved into a small, three-bedroom apartment. My father did not work for several months, cried at any mention of my mother, and spent a lot of time at home. Occasionally he would take off on strange trips with people I didn't know very well. He bought a leather jacket and a new car. And although he was proud I was maintaining my grades in school, and seemingly managing Mom's death well, he did not see me grieving. In reality, I was grieving the way my mother had taught me to do so thus far, but it was not my father's way, and so he was worried.

Dad had taken on so many new roles—house organizer, schedule keeper (not his forte), the rule enforcer (not his typical role), and, well, just the parent. Don't get me wrong, I have always learned a lot from my father, but he was never really the "enforcer" of the household in a technical sense. This was a transition that was challenging for us both. I love my father dearly and he is a phenomenal role model who has loved me unconditionally from the day I was born. He has always been there for me and taught me fabulous lessons in loyalty, empathy, compassion, and love. But my father is not my mom. It was my mom who offered guidance in managing schoolwork, making new friends and keeping old ones, and dealing with big life transitions.

And so with all of his conflicting new roles, and all the changes I had been encountering in my life, we had a lot of trouble communicating. And after a few months, I found it easier just to not approach subjects that were hard for us to talk about. After a while, it became a habit to avoid these topics in general, and it was not long before I had created strict rules for myself for what I could and couldn't talk about. My mom was a topic that I decided was never comfortable to talk about. Luckily, no one asked me much about it as time went on.

However, our family friend, whom I had called when my mom was ill, stepped up as a huge support system once my mom died. She offered guidance when I asked for it, but did not push or judge when I did not want to talk. And she helped keep me sane by offering a wise perspective on my life and offering the guidance I so craved. She even protected me, ready to go to battle for me at the drop of a hat.

It was probably six months after my mom died that I felt the first desires to talk about my mom and what had happened. The hype around her death had calmed down and changes were continuing to happen. I felt I had no one to talk to about them. During the summer before high school, I worked as a stable hand at a girls' camp and was able to open up to some of the older counselors at the camp. This worked as a great temporary source of support because I knew that regardless of what happened, my vulnerability would not return home with me at the end of the summer. A lot of things changed that summer. I started driver's education, my dad and I moved out of the apartment and into our new house, and I went on my first real date with a boy. But ever since the first few weeks after my mom died, I had found it more and more difficult to talk about anything serious with my father.

Excluding the rare moments when I reached out to family friends or to camp counselors, I became very secluded, and essentially ignored my grief for many years. Although I had convinced myself that I was fine (and in some ways I think the way I handled my situation was really the best I could do, given the resources I had), I spent most of my time in high school either working hard on schoolwork, or out riding horses. Horseback riding was more than a coping mechanism for me; it was an entire world of escapism, separate from the complications at home. But as I started to get a bit older, I gradually became aware of the fact that I had become an empty shell, not allowing myself to feel any serious emotions, for fear I would have to talk about them.

It was not until many months after I started college that I began to understand how to open up a little bit, though the experience was terrifying to me. I believe the change in me was only possible because of my change in environment. With the start of college, I was suddenly able to make new friends, explore lots of interests, and also have a bit of space from my father and my history at home.

I first started my healing and grieving process when I was forced to tell even just the basics of my story to my suite mates and my new friends, something I had never had to do before because I went to the same school for both middle and high school. In college I had a few friends who started to ask a lot more questions. Although I was tentative at first, I had a few persistent friends who continued to ask questions in a way that showed they really cared about me and were curious about where I was coming from. In my grieving process, I have never been one to become visibly emotional; I often hold my feelings in instead. One friend in particular didn't skip a beat in asking about my story and didn't shy away from talking about death and the hard topics. Gradually, I began to trust her and open up to her about my mom and the relationship with my dad, which I was working hard to repair, or at least better understand.

As I became more comfortable talking about my loss, I started healing and grieving a little bit at a time. I channeled a lot of my grief into journaling and artwork. But I still felt a gap inside, a place that my well-intentioned friends couldn't quite reach. There were many parts of my mother's illness and death that I was still processing. In a moment when my feelings had built up to a breaking point, I saw a counselor at our university's counseling center and poured everything out to her, crying more than I had in front of anyone in years. After helping me calm down, the counselor had me come back for a follow-up session. However, when I came back for the appointment I fell silent again. My façade was back up, and I insisted I didn't need any further counseling. It would be a year or more before I would see another counselor. Instead, I began actively seeking out others who shared a similar experience on the Internet. It was through this search that I learned the extent to which support groups can influence our outlook on life and impact our perception of the ability we have to bring about personal change.

It was a chance happening in the spring of my sophomore year that opened up my hidden gap inside. In a moment of loneliness, I sought out peer support through an online message board for "motherless daughters." I contacted another college student who had posted about the difficulties of transitioning to college without her mother. When she responded to my message, I was stunned to discover that she was also a student at UNC-Chapel Hill, where I was attending college. We agreed to meet up in person at a restaurant near campus. Though nervous to talk at first, we quickly found commonalities in the stories of losing our mothers and dealing with our fathers in the aftermath. As we became closer friends, I became compelled to reach out and find other students like us. Through a simple Google search, I found two organizations that would bring about an enormous change in my life: National Students of AMF, and Comfort Zone Camp.

National Students of AMF is a peer support network that supports college students who have a parent or close loved one who has died or is living with a chronic or terminal illness. Upon learning about this organization, my friend and I immediately contacted the founder to see if they had a chapter on our campus. There was not a chapter, so my friend and I started one. As I became more involved with the group and met a dozen or more fellow students working through grief, not only did my mental health improve, but I also gained energy and a renewed sense of purpose in my life. Having other people my age around who "got it" was also important for my taking ownership over my grieving process. With the confidence I gained through learning about grief and connecting with others who were experiencing or working with grief, I learned how to fill some of the gaps I felt. Although our losses were very different, we all shared a common bond.

Around the same time, I also began volunteering with Comfort Zone Camp, a bereavement camp for children who have experienced the loss of a close loved one. My work with Comfort Zone Camp is especially important to me. Not only do I feel fulfilled by supporting kids in a way I wish I could have been supported when my mom died, but I am also able to see myself in the kids I get to know. I find myself processing my past more than I ever have been able to, because of my weekends volunteering at camp.

As I became more involved with helping others and got to know people who were seeing mental health professionals and getting a lot out of the experience, I decided to give counseling another try. It was painfully awkward for me at first, because I did not know how to become vulnerable in front of a complete stranger. It took several sessions for me to warm up enough to the point where my heart was no longer racing and my face was not flush red the entire hour. And to this day, I still find it challenging to open up, although I have seen several counselors in the past few years. My experiences with counseling both through the university's counseling center as well as outside the university helped me forgive myself and find some peace from the confusion I had been feeling.

It has been a long and tumultuous 11 years since my mother died. Sometimes I feel I've lived three or four lives already. I know my healing journey has only just begun, and I still have much to learn. However, I also know that having the opportunity to open up, connect, and support others made a change in me that I will forever be grateful for.

Casey

Sex: Female

Age: 25

Time since death loss:
3 years, 2 months

Sick prior and died during college

Death loss: Father

Colorectal cancer

When I was a junior in high school, my dad was diagnosed with colorectal cancer; shortly thereafter, he underwent surgery and radiation and was deemed "in remission" shortly before I graduated from high school. Unfortunately for our family that was only the beginning of a very long journey with cancer.

In the fall of 2006, I enrolled at the University of Pennsylvania, moving nearly 3000 miles cross country from my hometown in Northern California. Though I loved this new coast, my transition to college was rocky. I sensed that I needed to be elsewhere, and that Christmas, I applied to transfer to some smaller colleges. But, a few months later, I received the phone call that changed everything. My dad had gone in for a routine check-up; the cancer was back, and this time it had spread to the lungs. The words "metastasized cancer" swirled in my head for weeks. At the end of the semester, I submitted my transfer paperwork and, thankfully, got into a college only an hour's flight from home.

That summer was the beginning of three years of intensive chemotherapy, ongoing appointments with the oncologist, and what felt like a never-ending period of waiting, waiting, waiting for the next test results. For two years, my dad slowly made his way through all available metastasized colorectal cancer chemotherapy cocktails, all while continuing to teach his beloved high school U.S. history.

When I started college that fall, this time as a transfer student, I already felt I was a world away from everyone else. I flew home often, Skyped frequently, and always felt one step removed from the rhythms of college life. Thankfully, I had transferred to a place

(Scripps College) that was a perfect fit for me, and it provided a community in which I felt safe, respected, and supported. My parents sensed that as well, and we knew it was where I needed to be in this journey.

As college inched along, I came to find that my stress and grief felt more manageable the more I could recede from view. At the start, I felt relieved telling my story and sharing the details of my home life. But, understandably, people rarely asked. It was uncomfortable, and it felt so dissonant from the vibrant life swirling around us. It eventually felt easier to spend time with a select group of people, and I avoided time in bigger groups. I wanted one-on-one time, so I could feel understood, loved, and a version of my old self. So, I carved out time to do just that, both with the friends who surrounded me and in the activities where I sought solace (and those moments of pure, in-the-moment joy).

One such place that became a weekly respite for me was Challah for Hunger. It was a nonprofit that began at Scripps, where students baked hundreds of loaves of challah each week, and the proceeds funded humanitarian efforts in Darfur. The loftier mission was inspiring, but I found the simple act of weekly baking had even deeper personal meaning. It got me out of my head, into a kitchen, and surrounded by like-minded friends. Those quiet moments, with only the oven buzzing behind me, made the rest of my world recede for a few hours. And, the routine—kneading dough, watching the braids rise, and providing a weekly treat for everyone on campus—made me feel more connected to my community than anything else.

As a transfer student, I also dove headfirst into the admissions office, where I worked as a tour guide (mastering the art of walking backwards) and eventually became an intern. Seeing our campus through prospective students' eyes was a constant reminder of the hopeful anticipation of high school, and the excitement of new college life. No matter how tumultuous my path had been, I adored my school, and those moments with new families reminded me why.

Though I loved how I spent my time, I found it to be in stark contrast from what I had enjoyed in high school (and what I envisioned college to be). This time around, I liked being behind the scenes. I didn't run for student government, gallivant in Berlin while studying art history, or attempt to make our basketball team (though I imagine that wouldn't have ended well). Partially I felt drained at the thought of the schedule I once kept. But I also enjoyed my new quieter life.

Most surprising of all, though, was that I developed a fairly motley crew of friends. I spent countless late nights with my best friend, and I found a supportive group of fellow transfer students. But my other close friends were not in my peer group at all—our Director of Admissions and my Women's Studies professor. Both of them became endless sources of light, wisdom, laughter, and compassion. They balanced conversations about the latest *Glee* episode with a discussion of chemo cocktails. It normalized everything. They also empathized to a higher degree than most: one's close friend was struggling with cancer, and the other had a son with Crohn's disease. Knowing that I had people familiar with the strangeness of grief and disease was a huge relief to me. Their offices became refuges, and I came to see them both as friends and mentors.

By the end of my junior year, my family was reaching the end of possible treatments for my dad. The cancer had been stalled by chemo for two years, but now it seemed to be growing. We began drafting plans to move to Germany temporarily for a well-reputed clinical trial. I made plans to delay a fellowship and dive into this new adventure (I had taken college German, after all). Alas, on the day of my last final of junior year, everything inexplicably changed.

My dad had been experiencing leg pain for a few days, and my parents decided to take him into critical care. I checked in with them before my Logic final, mostly focusing on being done with the most dreadful class of college, not thinking about this seemingly random hospital visit. I called two hours later in a celebratory mood. But my parents let me know that my dad had been admitted to the hospital, and the on-call doctor was afraid his pain could be something more serious.

In a sober yet tentatively joyful mood, my best friend and I picked up McDonald's and camped out on her dorm room floor to watch an old episode of *30 Rock*. My car was packed for my journey home the next day, so all we did was wait. Shortly before 8pm, my mom called. Immediately, I knew—it was that dire thing we did not want to talk about. He had been admitted to surgery, and the doctor deemed this procedure potentially fatal. In perhaps the fastest and most surreal 90 minutes of my life, I sprinted to a cab, rushed to the airport, and (thankfully) got on the last flight to San Jose. Family friends picked me up from the airport and, in silence, drove me to the surgery waiting room of our second home, El Camino Hospital.

My mom was alternatively pacing and sitting in the corner, holding hands with our dear family friend. After two hours, we had no new information. Minutes inched by. Finally, the surgeon emerged; my dad was alive, but the situation was grave. My dad had what is called necrotizing fasciitis—what we (crudely) call "flesh eating bacteria." Somehow, a fissure had developed in my dad's colon, and bacteria had slowly leaked into his bloodstream. In surgery, they were able to stop the spread. However, much of his leg was already compromised, and they had to remove most of his left thigh and buttock.

We lived in the hospital for the majority of that summer, as my dad relearned how to sit up, stand, and—eventually—walk with a walker. Of course, we quickly learned that with the amount of devastation the fasciitis caused, he could never undergo chemotherapy again. Killing cells was the opposite of what he needed. Many days we discussed—in a somewhat darkly awed tone—how we never envisioned flesh-eating bacteria being the thing that would do him in. But, each day, a new string of former students, friends, or family would come visit him, and he became a floor favorite of the nurses. With all of that support, and my dad's fervent interest in keeping my own history research alive, I left for my fellowship in Philadelphia for a month. Each night, I would call him to share what I found in the archive that day, conversations that took us out of the building gloom of what was to come.

When I returned, my dad was discharged from the hospital, and we began to enlist the help of at home nurses and hospice care. We put a list on the fridge of to do's—walking around the block, going to his favorite coffee shop, and attending a James Taylor concert. My senior year seemed worlds away.

A week before classes began, the hospice estimated that he had only a few weeks' time left. My dad would simply not let me miss going back, and since I was graduating early, this was my last semester. Thankfully, Scripps was incredibly accommodating. My classes were only Monday to Wednesday, allowing me to be home five nights a week. For the first few weeks of the semester, my dad eagerly listened to my developing thesis prospectus. Then, after a Wednesday flight home at the end of September, he had trouble breathing. He didn't move from his hospice bed. By Friday night, he fell into a restless sleep. One day later, he passed away, my mom and I by his side.

After years of envisioning a world without him, I realized that waking up in a world without someone is one of the most universal heartaches. And one of the strangest feelings. That morning, my mom and I went to the beach, picked up some pumpkins at a farm, and laughed and cried. I went back to school a few days later, but I stuck to the same fly-home schedule to help plan the memorial service.

Returning to college after that day was like entering a veiled world. I finished my semester, but it was a blur of paper writing, ice cream eating, and deep aching. When I returned six months later to walk across the stage at graduation, I felt the sting of that empty chair in the audience. But I also knew how proud he'd be. And, as I watched my sea-foam-green robed classmates march across that stage, reflecting on our years on this campus, I reminded myself that was all that mattered.

Questions for Reflection

Please reflect on and/or write out answers to the following questions:

1.   What ways, if any, have you used to remain connected with or to memorialize your loved one? What might be some new ways that you could do so?

2.   What can you do to help someone else to memorialize a loved one? How could you help them generate activities that would be particularly meaningful for them?

3.   In what ways, if any, have you found that helping others or doing community service has helped you in your grief journey?

4.   In what ways, if any, have you grieved more actively? How do you believe these approaches have served to help you take a break and/or express your grief?

5.   How might you be both intuitive and instrumental in your grief? How can you use these ideas in moving forward with your grief?

For supporters:

> How might you help grieving college students and young adults consider creative ways to memorialize a loved one who has died?

CHAPTER 3

Forced Maturity

Teenagers and young adults who experience grief often describe a sense that they have aged or been forced to mature beyond their years (Kuntz, 1991). Our authors often perceived themselves as more mature than their non-grieving peers. This idea was not usually a judgment of their peers being immature, but rather another explanation for why the grievers felt so different and unable to connect with their peers. They described believing that their peers could not truly understand the depth of their grief or the added responsibility, worry, and required divided attention that comes with the experience of family illness and/or death. Their peers "didn't get" how fragile and unpredictable life truly is.

Young adults are often called upon to serve in caregiving roles for their ill loved ones and are also more highly involved in formal memorial planning and other critical post-death decisions than children and adolescents. Although they may welcome these opportunities to contribute to their families and loved one, they are also in some ways torn—they do not want these types of responsibilities.

Most authors described a decreased desire to "go out all the time" and difficulty relating to and integrating into the carefree environment of college life, or at least the carefree attitude that most students display. They often commented about the reality that they were not having and were not going to have the same college experience as their peers. They also expressed occasional frustration with peers who, in a way, had the luxury of worrying about the typical college stresses, such as grades and "annoying" parents. It is important to note that in some narratives (in other chapters) the authors described an approach of focusing on college life as an initial way of distancing themselves from the reality of their grief. It was a welcome distraction at the time, but at least one author shared some reservations about the choices she made while grieving in a culture often focused on drinking.

As noted earlier, there are likely many college students who have experienced death losses and likely many peers who could relate to each other's feelings of separateness. But without a clear way to identify or connect with others with similar experiences, students are left feeling different and often set apart. It's not considered cool to be the "old guy" or "Debby Downer" in college, so many students hide the feelings that would bring about these stereotypes.

We have included the following two stories that we believe demonstrate the sense of forced maturity often present for grieving college students and young adults.

Patrick

Sex: Male

Age: 21

Time since death loss: 1 year, 10 months

Sick prior and died during college

Death loss: Mother

Amyotrophic lateral sclerosis

My name is Patrick Cho, I'm 21 years old and a senior at Center College in Danville, KY. As a college senior, "adulthood" is just around the corner. For most people the moment they "grow up" is when they walk across the stage and get their college diploma. For me, that moment was two years ago, when my parents told me my mother had amyotrophic lateral sclerosis (ALS) or Lou Gehrig's disease.

ALS patients begin to lose fine motor skills with their hands like writing, or driving, before losing control of their limbs. Eventually, victims can't walk, feed or bathe themselves, or dress themselves. As the disease progresses, patients can't speak or communicate, and eventually suffocate to death. Lou Gehrig's is a horrible illness, and carries with it not only appalling suffering in itself but also an enormous burden of caregiving on loved ones. That experience of caregiving, combined with the actual loss of my mother, was far beyond the experience of any of my peers.

One of the hardest parts of Mom's illness was a feeling of isolation—I didn't know anyone my own age who had experienced anything remotely like what I was going through. I felt disconnected and listless. I desperately wanted to reach out to friends and classmates my own age, yet whenever I did so I felt bitter, unsatisfied, and a little angry. Whenever I talked to friends, their stories of classes and hanging out on the weekend felt like tales from another planet. Social media didn't help—constant Facebook updates about papers, parties, or fantastic study abroad experiences only added to the sense of separation. I was envious and resentful of my friends, yet felt guilty for feeling so. Many tried to sympathize, but our conversations fell flat as each of us had a hard time relating to one another. It was so hard to relate to my friends that I became increasingly frustrated trying to bridge the gap. As time wore on I deliberately cut myself off from most of my peers and friends—I just didn't have anything to talk with them about. This strategy only made me feel even more isolated and frustrated, leading to a destructive cycle of emotion.

The other main emotion I remember is guilt. The burden of caregiving was unlike anything I or my father had ever experienced before. Every day was the same as the one before it, and I began to dread waking up in the morning knowing what the day would be like even before it began.

Every day we would get up, help Mom go to the bathroom, get dressed, brush her teeth, go make food and then come back upstairs to feed it to her. Then I was in her room for the rest of the day to help her with whatever she might need (e.g., moving limbs, giving medicine). Because she was in constant pain, we had to give her pain medicine every four hours, day and night, which meant that all of us were sleep deprived for over a year. I had never been so regularly exhausted, and if *I* was tired that was nothing compared with my father. We were 24-hour caregivers for a year and a half, and not once did I ever see him become short or irritable with Mom.

Despite constant sleep interruption, despite still having to work from home, despite having to do some physically exhausting work lifting and moving Mom in bed and in chairs, he was unfailingly patient and kind, though I know he felt frustrated. I honestly don't know how he did it—there were times when I was irritable and bad tempered with both of them. As time went on I felt increasingly jittery, resentful, sometimes wishing this whole thing was over. Then I remembered my struggle as a caregiver was nothing compared to Mom's suffering, and an enormous sense of guilt would wash over me.

Mom's attitude didn't help that guilt, because she was never reproachful or demanding. Her main concern seemed to be how Dad and I were going to deal with her death, and how she could make caring for her easier. She demanded we take time off to go out of the house, to have time to ourselves, to relax—I have no idea how she managed to be so understanding. Even as her body failed and she was forced to rely on us for virtually everything, she always tried to be optimistic. There were times when her sense of humor would still shine through. As she began to lose control of her hands, her joints stiffened and her fingers began to lock into place. On her right hand, it happened that all her fingers but one had curved inward, leaving her middle finger rigid. She laughed and feebly moved her arm, saying, "It's a good thing I can't drive anyway, cause with this hand I'd get into a lot of trouble!"

I would tell this story to friends and usually there was initial laughter followed by hesitation: *Can I laugh at this? Isn't everything related to death supposed to be serious? Did I do something wrong?* Confronting this lack of understanding about death became another part of the grieving process.

Losing a loved one is one of the most difficult times in someone's entire life, and can bring out the best and worst in yourself and your friends. During Mom's illness and especially afterwards, I grew familiar with the awkward encounters, the perfunctory, "I'm sorry" or, "If there's anything I can do," and people avoiding my eyes and shuffling away as quickly as possible. Others avoided mentioning it at all, and looked panic stricken and uncomfortable, whenever even a passing reference to Mom's death came up. I was surprised at how universal this reaction was—not only my college friends who had no experience of death, but even full adults who had lost loved ones were equally stumped at how to react.

For all the obligatory sympathy, there were many friends who were extraordinarily caring and kind. One family friend immediately flew across the country on hearing the news; others consistently messaged me with little thoughts of kindness, all the more thoughtful because I usually ignored their contacts. For the most part, however, neither my acquaintances nor I knew how to interact with one another. In a way, both of us were yearning for a guide, a playbook telling us what we were each supposed to say and how we were to act. Death is so rarely talked about that no one quite knew what the rules were.

There's a disconnect between the way death and dying is portrayed in the media and real experience. The stereotypical image of death as bedside reunions where old wounds are forgiven, of dignified funerals where people are tastefully sad doesn't always fit with real experience. Grief isn't so quaint and picturesque—it's ugly and brutal and scarring. I don't believe there are many tricks to help you "move on," no orderly progression through stages of grief. You just…go on, lose yourself in life, and try not to forget the person you lost and what they meant to you. As time passes there are other things to keep you occupied and the overwhelming grief isn't always at the forefront of your mind, until at some point it's not the first thing you think about as you wake. Eventually memories fade, but I am still surprised at the power and intensity of grief—a song, a smell can provoke a memory and a wave of grief washes over you as overwhelming as the day it happened.

Mom died in March 2011, a little over 18 months after she was first diagnosed. Losing a loved one causes you to think about life's fundamental questions—death, loss, afterlife. One of my favorite books is by Thornton Wilder called *The Bridge of San Luis Rey*. I read an excerpt from it at Mom's funeral. The book is about life, and the meaning of death, and at the end Wilder pretty much sums up how I feel. He writes:

> But soon we shall die, and all memory of those five will have left the earth, and we ourselves shall be loved for a while and forgotten. But the love will have been enough; all those impulses of love return to the love that made them. Even memory is not necessary for love. There is a bridge between the land of the living and the land of the dead and the bridge is love, the only survival, the only meaning.

Patricia

Sex: Female

Age: 29

Time since death loss: 8 years, 11 months

During college

Death loss: Father

Heart attack

In the winter of my junior year of college, my father died suddenly of a heart attack. We had seen each other for Christmas Eve and I returned to my mother's house on Christmas morning (my parents are divorced). At approximately 2am on the morning he died, I was awakened suddenly by a sharp pain in my chest. It was excruciating, but just for a moment. Two hours later I received the call to say my father had died at around the same time I felt that jolt. I found that experience, in some ways, to be incredibly comforting to me following his death. I felt as if I had "felt" him when he died, as if we communicated somehow in that moment.

Since I'm an only child, I was responsible for planning my dad's funeral. I was lucky enough to have some of my father's good friends pay for his funeral, along with donations received at his funeral; otherwise, I have no idea how I would have handled the cost, as he had no savings and no insurance policy. The determination to cremate him was made, in part, due to expense (which made me feel ridiculous and like a bad daughter), and also because I had no idea where to put him. I wanted him close to me, and the idea of having him buried in some random plot just seemed wrong. With the help of family and friends, we packed his house before the new year and vacated.

I reached out to my friends and faculty through email to let them know that he had died and I had not yet determined whether I would be returning to school. My two favorite professors called. Both encouraged me to return. One, who was much like a father to me, said, "Your father would not want this to upset your college career. And, frankly, we need you." I think the last statement was the most powerful. After my dad's death, I really needed a purpose and it felt good to be needed and to have a focus.

I spoke with the head of the resident life program and asked for permission to return to campus early to get accustomed to being there. I felt like I needed to get settled and determine what I was going to say to people. I also needed some distance from all of the family members who were hovering around me, and from the constant memories.

My friends tried very hard to relate and I appreciated that. But I also found that people avoided talking about him because they didn't want me to be sad, which, sometimes, was the opposite of what I wanted. I also found myself pulling away from my friends because my emotions were unpredictable. For example, I saw a funny movie that I thought my dad would have liked and started bawling. I didn't want to burden anyone with that.

Mostly I was frustrated. I attended a counseling session at my university's counseling center. The counselor told me I was in the "denial" stage as I explained that, sometimes, I would expect to see him or get a phone call from him. I was not in denial. I had prepared his funeral, stood at his open casket, and packed all of his earthly possessions. I just desperately missed him. I didn't want to be categorized, especially with categories that didn't fit. I also went to a group counseling session at the hospital, but that involved older adults who had lost elderly parents or young children. I struggled to relate. I couldn't find support groups online. I couldn't find books particular to my needs as a young adult. I became angry.

There came a point in college when I felt like my identity as a person who had lost her father had nearly taken over who I was. It was part of everything I did. I talked about it. I presented on it. When I accepted scholarships, it was part of my speech. I also found myself developing co-dependent relationships with friends to fill that void. I think some friends felt that I was using it to manipulate people. I think that could be true. In a lot of ways it was a weapon. People couldn't understand how I felt and I wanted them to know that. I wanted them to hurt by showing my hurt, since that would be as close as we could come to understanding each other. That lasted for a short period of time. Then I felt ready to incorporate the grief into who I am, rather than allowing it to define me.

My sociology advisor encouraged me to focus on "grief during college" for my senior thesis. What started as a literature review turned into interviews with college students who had lost loved ones—everyone from partners to parents, many of whom had been sick and died while the students were in school. Few had told their friends or the school about the deaths. It was so nice to speak with people about their experiences. While the loved one lost may not have been the same, the feelings associated with the losses were at least familiar. Finding that group of people turned out to be the best way for me to cope with my feelings of listlessness. The experience grounded me, gave my grief a purpose and allowed me to make something positive out of this life-changing loss. I completed my thesis and presented it at my university. It was incredibly empowering.

Since his death, my memory of him has faded, especially his voice which is the most difficult for me to lose. Thankfully, I do have some videos of him. I think of him less often, though frequently still talk to him about problems and when I need a source of strength. I channel him, I guess you'd say. In the past two years, I have forgotten the anniversary of his death and likely would have this year were it not for writing this story. The forgetting tends to make me feel like I am not honoring his memory.

Milestones are difficult. It's still difficult for me to watch father–daughter dances at weddings, as he wasn't there for mine. I bawled when I danced with my stepdad; I felt, again, as if I was disrespecting his honor by dancing with my stepdad. It was difficult when my husband and I bought our first house. It was difficult when we got a cat, because my father loved cats. And, sometimes, it just creeps up on me suddenly, in the middle of nothing in particular; I will feel a profound sense of loss in not having him around for the mundane. That, I am certain, will never go away.

Questions for Reflection

Please reflect on and/or write out answers to the following questions:

1. In what ways, if any, do you believe you matured in connection with the death of your loved one?

2. What were particular elements of the death that your peers could just not understand? Who was able to understand?

For supporters:

> What can you do to better relate to the college students and young adults you are seeking to support? How can you acknowledge the ways their death losses may have required them to mature?

CHAPTER 4

Importance of Connecting with Grieving Peers

Support from others who are also grieving is important for many grievers (Parkes and Prigerson, 2009). Possibly related to our method of collecting the narratives through AMF, all of the authors mentioned the importance of interacting with other grieving peers. In some cases, even one conversation appeared to make a big difference for them. For others, just the knowledge of the existence of even one other grieving peer on campus seemed to provide relief. For most, it was the power of mutual understanding that emerged through conversations with grieving peers.

Students noted the freedom that came from not having to explain everything and the comfort and normalcy that came with being in a setting where they did not have to always monitor themselves (e.g., avoiding mentioning the loved one who died, not allowing tears to rise). The freedom to talk openly about their loved one at one moment and to laugh about a funny movie at the next was meaningful. There was no need to filter because grieving peers knew the variable nature of grief—and there was no sense of judgment or expectation of expression.

Though it was clear that the connection with grieving peers was important for our authors, it was also clear that it is not easy to identify other grieving peers. Few college students or young adults self-identify or disclose their grief experiences until someone else does. For many of the authors, their opportunity to connect with a grieving peer came through joining a peer-led grief support group or participating in a community service project. Unfortunately, these opportunities are often limited on college campuses and possibly even more so for young adults following college.

As we discussed in Chapter 1, social media does provide the possibility for instant "connections" with a large number of others; however, our authors offered conflicting reports about the depth of connection that can occur through virtual means. We hope that additional, more meaningful, connections can be developed through social media so that the benefit of connecting with grieving peers can be experienced by more young adults.

We have included the following three stories that we believe illustrate the importance of connecting with grieving peers for grieving college students and young adults.

Margaret

Sex: Female

Age: 28

Time since death loss:
2 years, 2 months

After college

Death loss: Mother

Cancer

Although losing my mother after college was the most difficult thing I have ever had to go through, losing my only remaining grandparents in college was similarly difficult for me. I am not sure if it was losing my grandparents or the complete dissolution of my extended family, but I blocked out all of my emotions from those losses all throughout college. I realize now that some of the behaviors that I regret from college are eerily similar to how I have dealt with the grief connected with my mother's death. After my grandparents died, I stopped going to class. I went out to more parties and stayed out later. I avoided trying my best (at anything) for fear of failure. It was easy to say, "I didn't do well on that test because I didn't try." It would have been much harder if I had taken personal responsibility for not being good enough.

The summer after my sophomore year, I traveled throughout Europe with my sister and learned a lot about myself, as clichéd as it sounds. I became more focused on my goal to do well in school. I looked into building my resumé and engaged in more volunteer activities to keep myself involved in my community. I also met my husband-to-be that summer. He helped push me to do my best and to not settle for second best. College is full of friends and great times but only some friends are truly the sort of people who are there for you in your time of need. College is meant to be a fun and happy time and it is hard to bring up difficult times with your friends. For me in particular it was hard to talk about my grandparents passing away that summer. I didn't want to come back to school shouting it from the rooftops. "Hey everyone! I had to hold my grandmother's hand as she stopped breathing." It just wasn't something I really felt like talking about.

One year after I graduated from college, my mother was diagnosed with a malignant brain tumor, glioblastoma multiforme. At the time, I was working at the Brain Tumor Center at Duke and this situation was just so difficult for me to take on. I had been watching patients not survive this disease for the last year. I knew what this disease did to other patients and I was so scared to think of my mother in that position. My parents got divorced when I was young and my mother never remarried, so I was deemed the primary caregiver. My sister moved home from New York City and my other sister, living in Atlanta, traveled up and back on weekends, taking time off to be home. I continued my full-time job after a few months off to help get my mother settled into her treatment. I felt most helpful being at the Brain Tumor Center and trying to get her the best care possible. This was so challenging as I was the only one in my family in the medical field and everyone had questions about everything. I felt inept and struggled with having to be stoic.

My mother did not take the treatment well and quickly became very frail. She was unable to see out of the right side of both eyes so she was no longer able to drive. She felt uncomfortable in crowds and anywhere her vision felt like a disability. She was irritated by her lack of independence after raising three strong independent women on her own. I was irritated with the situation and often got irritated with my sisters, husband-to-be, and even my mother when things got tough. Everyone was stressed and often tempers flared. We tried to live life as normally as possible. We went on like this for a full year. I got married, my sister got married, and my other sister got a great job in New York and moved back.

After a year, my mom's tumor recurred and things went downhill from there. My mother was placed on hospice less than six months later and my sisters both came back home. We spent around the clock hours with my mother and decisions became much more difficult. I never imagined talking with my mother, aged 53, about what she wanted her funeral to look like. Watching my mother die was the hardest thing I have ever had to do.

For most of the first few months following my mother's death, I was trying to ignore what had happened. I tried to avoid things that would remind me of her. I was unable to really talk about it for quite some time. I couldn't even say it out loud. For some reason, that was always the most difficult for me. "My mother just passed away." I think it took me six months to be able to say it without choking up. The avoidance transferred into other areas of my life. I avoided important things and procrastinated tasks. I let my life pass me by. I used my mother's illness as an excuse for not doing well. I decided to take the Medical College Admission Test (MCAT) when I knew wasn't ready and applied to medical school even though I knew my application wasn't good enough yet.

The only thing I seemed to be motivated to do was get my mother's house on the market and distribute her things among my siblings. Living in her house with all of her things was very difficult for me. I needed a fresh start. I needed to get away from looking at my old life in our old home. It is strange to think back, that I could avoid everything else in my life, but this was something I set my mind to doing.

I was sad and angry about what had happened. I was angry that so many selfish people in this world who cared nothing about others were still living when my mother, a sweet and caring person, was not. She had devoted her life to me and my sisters; what did she do to deserve dying so young and in such pain? As a healthcare professional, this is one of the hardest feelings for me to shake.

I was sad that I would not be able to share so many things with my mother. I was sad that we wouldn't have any more annual family vacations. I was sad that I would likely see much less of my sisters due to them being so far away and not having a common area to come together. Then there was the guilty feeling. I thought there were times when I was selfish and could have been there more for my mother during her illness. Did I make the right decisions on her healthcare? Did I do my best? It is hard to tell yourself that you did everything you could when all you can think about is a petty fight or a time when you just wanted to do something a normal 24-year-old would be doing. It made it even more difficult as everyone was continually praising me for being such a good caregiver. It is much easier to focus on one fight than years of caregiving. Did I comfort her enough? Could I have done more for her? Did we pick the right treatment? Did we force her to keep fighting when she had had enough? Questions that will never be able to be answered...

My social life was the most helpful and meaningful part of my life during my grief journey. Getting out and leaving my mother's house allowed me to experience things that normal 24-year-olds were experiencing. Sure, it was difficult at times because deep down I was still upset, but feeling normal if only for a night helped tremendously. I think it may have been getting out of feeling so much sympathy for myself and from everyone around me. It was like a cloud lifting off of me for a brief moment. It was activities like going to a sporting event, going to a movie, or even just going over to a friend's house for dinner.

When I lost my mother, I was taking the paramedic academy with Lenoir Community College. The academy was about eight months and we were all told from the very beginning that if you missed an on-campus class then you would be kicked out of the class. I assumed this would not hold true for extreme situations. I was taking this class during my mother's illness and as her healthcare power of attorney needed to be there for her in the end of her life. My mother slipped into a coma the night before one of our classes and the hospice nurse believed she would not make it 24 hours. I emailed my teacher that I would not make it and asked him what I could do to make the class up. He reminded me of the policy. The policy seemed absurd to me at the time and still does today. I couldn't even begin to deal with being kicked out of an eight-month program in the last two months. I sent my professor a reply email that stated my frustrations. I couldn't believe what they were putting me through when my mother was dying right before me.

After I told my aunt in the NC State Legislature about what I had encountered at a state-funded institution she helped get me in contact with their liaison to the community colleges. I was able to tell her about my situation and the case was reviewed by the president of the community college. He was unaware of this policy and asked that the Emergency Medical Services (EMS) program reassess my case. I was eventually let back into the program but I always felt like they resented how I went about fixing my problem. I honestly didn't want to deal with it but my aunt didn't want me to regret that decision later on in life. I am so glad that I did not let all that hard work disappear. I love being a paramedic today and providing medical care has given me the drive to fulfill my goal of becoming a more advanced healthcare provider. I am currently applying to Physician Assistant programs.

Almost six months after my mom died, I attended a conference focused on college student grief. I had been involved for many years with the organization that hosted the conference but really didn't realize how much three minutes of sharing my story could do for me. I had been taking minutes all day for the conference until eventually we got together to show the college students how the peer-led support group usually worked. We went around the circle telling our stories. It was time for me to share mine and I told a room full of new friends what I had gone through. It was liberating. I don't know what had been holding me back for so long! I don't know what it was about letting it out but I think it had something to do with whom I was talking. I had obviously told people before but I think the common ground we all shared of losing someone made me feel heard and not pitied. I felt as if people understood what I was saying and what I had gone through. I knew everyone's situation was very different but having a shared experience can go a long way to just not feeling so alone.

The most effective talks I have had have been with friends who have gone through similar experiences. People came out of the woodwork to tell me about what they had been through and how they had made it through it. It was comforting to know I was not the only one this was happening to. This helps keep the angry feelings down; I know that it has not just happened to me.

Even though I feel that I have shared my grief story and have healed from the loss of my mother, often life experiences bring that loss right back to the front of my mind. Being pregnant is a good example of this. I am reminded again of petty fights I had with my mother as a teenager and when she was sick. I can safely say that I never understood how much a parent loves their child until I got pregnant. I have so much more respect for my mother than I ever had before and I will never be able to tell her that. It also widens the void I feel with her loss. Everyone constantly asks, "Your mother must be so excited?!" I can't get upset with them because how would they know, but it is difficult to have this reminder of my loss so often. In birth classes, all the girls talk about how great their relationships are with their mother now that they are experiencing pregnancy. It is just a constant reminder that these are things that I will never experience.

Alex

Sex: Female

Age: 20

Time since death loss: 2 years

During college

Death loss: Father

Heart attack

It was like any other Christmas Eve, but I distinctly remember every single moment like it was yesterday. I had just celebrated my 18th birthday a few days before and had finished my first semester of college. My family has a tradition of opening presents on Christmas Eve, and as usual, I was out shopping with my sister for the gifts we were planning on opening that night. My mom was at work all morning, and my dad was at home by himself. The whole time he was hurrying my mom, my sister, and me to get home because Christmas was his favorite holiday.

Once everyone was home, we had our usual Christmas Eve dinner. My dad sat on his favorite chair and watched his favorite movie, *National Lampoon's Christmas Vacation*, as my sister and I cleaned our rooms. It was a rule that our rooms had to be spotless (the only way my mom could get us to clean our rooms) before we could open presents. My dad usually never came upstairs, but on this particular night he did, as if he was saying goodbye. Before long, I was back cleaning my room hoping to finish before it got too late. Everything seemed very normal.

Then I overheard my mom asking my dad if he wanted her to call an ambulance. I quickly rushed downstairs to find my dad still sitting in his chair. I kissed his head and then watched as paramedics rushed into my house. No one will ever compare to my dad for the amount of humor he exhibited in any situation. Even during a moment like this, my dad joked, "Now don't forget to take me to the hospital." But the image that will remain in my mind for the rest of my life is my dad being wheeled away into the ambulance. I looked at my dad, expecting to see a sick man, but I saw just the opposite. He gave me one of the biggest grins I have ever seen on his face. He acted as if he was royalty being carried in a chariot. I said the words, "Bye dad, love you," as if I was going to see him when he got back. My dad suffered a major heart attack in the ambulance on the way to the hospital and my last glimpse of him was his warm smile. I never had time to prepare for his death, gather last words to say to him, or to have a goodbye moment.

Shortly after my dad left for the hospital, my uncle called us to tell us that he was picking us up. At this point we were unaware of what had happened. We assumed we were going to his house to stay the night, but he said we were going to the hospital. That's when my mind was redirected to all the possible things that could be wrong. But every time death crossed my mind, I quickly brushed it off because I knew it could not be true.

We walked down a long white hallway toward a room labeled 30. Just when I thought we were going to walk in there to see my dad, we were redirected to a holding room next door. My mom was waiting for us at the door. She held us close and whispered, "Your father is no longer with us." My heart completely dropped. I could hear my sister's screams in the background, but I quietly walked to the corner and my body sunk. Someone carried me to the couch where I sat for hours, sobbing, hazily watching as family members came in and out till it was Christmas morning.

I was still planning to head back to Lewis in a few weeks to finish my second semester of freshman year. In my time left at home, I went through the motions of life. Our house was constantly filled with family members, meals that had been made for us, and many flowers and cards. None of that even fazed me. Since the moment I came home from the hospital, I wrote about my dad, my feelings, and what I was going through. I was never one to keep a journal or diary, but in this particular moment I wanted to write down everything about my dad, as if I didn't want to forget all the things I loved about him.

When it was time for the funeral, my uncle asked me if I wanted to speak. My initial reaction was no, due to my fear of public speaking. But as I began to think over this opportunity in front of me, I decided to honor my father by telling everyone that day of how much my dad had meant to me; he was my best friend and biggest cheerleader in life. I couldn't think of the words to say that would illustrate the kind of man my dad was; he was too funny, generous, and kind to put into words. No words would describe my dad better than the memories that I had reminisced on for days, so I took my journal and compiled all the entries I had made into a speech that painted a beautiful picture of him. The day of the funeral, nothing will ever describe the feeling I experienced talking in front of over 500 people. I expected to be nervous, but I recall having a smile on my face the entire time, as if I was in conversation with my dad.

When I returned back at school for my second semester of freshman year, only two weeks after my dad had passed away, everything seemed to be where I left it. I did my normal routine of school, soccer practice, and library. Day in and day out, things didn't really seem out of the ordinary. I had felt comfortable being at home, so I never thought that being at school would be any different.

Within a few weeks, once my schoolwork began to pile up, and practices became more demanding; that is when everything in my world seemed to flip upside down. I started missing classes, and began going out more to distract myself. The more I tried to distract myself, the more I realized the feelings I was having weren't something that I could neglect. It was around that time that everything that had happened in the past month hit me. It was like I woke up and realized that my life was never going to be the same. I decided that the best decision for myself was to address these feelings and no longer try to mask them. I took time off from soccer to focus on myself, and sought out the counseling staff.

In counseling I finally found a place where I could openly talk about my dad and not get the "look" of pity. I had never been one to cry, but after my dad passed away, one of the best reliefs was to cry. I began calling them a "good cry" to denote them as a sign of relief. The lady I began talking to told me she had lost her dad when she was about my age. She actually knew what I was going though.

I also have a professor who has been one of the greatest mentors I have ever had. On any given time or day, I can go into his office to laugh, cry, scream, or vent. Not only has he been an open ear to me, but has always offered a word of encouragement. Whenever he says, "I am so proud of you," no words can describe what I feel inside. I guess this reminded me a lot of my dad, since he was my biggest support system. He would be on the sidelines cheering at practices, games, and making frequent calls to see how my grades were. After my dad passed, I felt so alone. I always had that one person I could count on for reassurance. Although no one can ever replace my dad, having a mentor who saw the success that I was making and who also cheered me on was a big relief for me.

One of most positive things I learned was to surround myself with friends who could keep an eye on me; not necessarily as babysitters, but people who were always there for me. Being in college is tough not having immediate family nearby, so creating a family of my own was the next best thing I could do. When I first went back to school I thought I could handle the things I could before. On the outside I tried to pretend like I was feeling OK. I would stamp a permanent smile on my face just long enough to make it back to my room and then cry once I got back. Going to a relatively small university, it was shocking that most of my classmates didn't even know my dad just died. I felt the need to fill up my day with as much stuff as I could to keep preoccupied. I felt the need to distract myself from reality. I started hanging out with people who didn't know what happened so that they wouldn't ask me. None of that solved anything. My good friends became my conscience. They would encourage a movie night or take me to have a study party in the library instead. Even though they might not have lost someone, having people who guided me and who wanted the best for me is what allowed me to occupy my time in a healthy way.

Another important aspect, in my opinion, is being able to talk about the person you lost. Talking about my dad and painting a picture of him for every person I talk to is what helps me. If I had gone the route of masking my feelings and avoiding conversations about him, then I would never be where I am at now. I was very hesitant to the idea of counseling. In my mind, I imagined bonsai trees, Zen gardens, and a long couch to lay on, mostly from what I had seen in movies. One day I decided to break through my negative connotation of counseling and see it first-hand.

Similar to having a counselor was talking to my peers who had also experienced loss. When someone close to you dies, you suddenly become more aware of other people who have lost someone. I would describe some of my closer friends as people who have dealt with grief first-hand. We aren't close because we have known each other for years or hang out every day, but having something like loss and grief as a commonality among two people brings them closer than any other aspect. Students may want to talk to someone who understands and "gets it," but may want to avoid all the pressures of going to a counselor. Some of my most memorable moments with my friends who have also lost their dads have been when they have knocked on my door to ask me a question and then ended up spending an hour talking: talking about the funny things that my dad used to say or how good of an athlete their dad was.

Death isn't something that is openly talked about and doesn't just affect one person. Breaking this barrier and showing that it is OK to talk about loss and connecting people who have gone through grief is so important.

Danielle B.

Sex: Female

Age: 23

Time since death loss:
9 years, 3 months

Prior to college

Death loss: Father

Diabetes—extended complications

Memories of my father have always been kept close to my heart. The relationship we had was so special. My parents divorced when I was six years old and so the time we spent together was cherished.

My dad was always honest about the status of his health; from a young age I knew he was sick. My dad was diagnosed with type 2 diabetes when he was 18 years old. As time passed, his condition worsened. Each new day was a blessing. Slowly his organs started to fail and with short notice he went on dialysis. Then he began to seize. I was home at the time of my father's first seizure. My younger sister and I were without any other adults in the house and so I made the call for help. Waiting for the ambulance felt like an eternity. Help could not arrive fast enough. My dad was released from the hospital with hopes of this being his first and last seizure. However, within the next six weeks, he was in and out of the emergency room. After his third visit to the hospital, the doctors decided to admit him. In the hospital he caught pneumonia and a week later passed away.

Because my dad was sick I started grieving for him before he passed away. I started to take great pride in my academics because it was an aspect of life that I could control at a time when a lot was out of reach. Every day I woke up with a pang in my heart. I often wished my dad's fight would end because I could not stand the thought of knowing he was going to die at any moment but was still fighting. Every time the phone rang, especially late at night, my stomach turned. *When would it happen, when would this end?* I stopped hanging out with friends after school and on the weekends. I could not laugh and play knowing my dad was no longer going to be in my life. It was all I could think about. I had difficulty talking about my father's death with others and so kept this experience within my family and closest friends at the time. No one I knew had had a similar event to mine and so I did not know anyone who "got it." Schoolwork instead consumed my life because excelling within the classroom took my mind off of what was going on at home.

I felt relieved when he was laid to rest. The struggle had come to an end after years of pain. Not a day goes by where I do not think about him. Milestones and special occasions are the hardest but I know he is with me every step of the way.

The night my father died my mom suggested I call my closest friends and tell them the news. One of the girls insisted on coming over that night, even though it was after 11pm. I waited for her on the front steps of my house. I do not know why I was so eager to see her that night. The moment she hugged me I fell apart again, an instance that was to happen too many times over the following weeks. She stayed at my house with her dad until 1am. It meant the world to see a friend care so much. At school the next day she had all my teachers sign a card for me. It made it easier for me to know I had her to help me through my days at school when I was away from my mom. I can never thank her enough for coming to my house that night and for being there with me when I needed her the most.

After my dad passed away I was in a series of long-term relationships. I felt comforted by the male affection after losing such attention from my father. During my senior year of high school I started a new relationship. My boyfriend at the time was hesitant and sensitive, and so in the beginning of our relationship I tried *not* to talk with him about my grief at all. However, as time passed I realized that in order to move forward with our relationship I needed to share my experience with him as well as the accompanying emotions. I started to tell stories, good and bad, about the times I had with my dad before he passed away. At first he did not have anything to say but I figured that the topic of death and grief is heavy and overwhelming, not to mention uncomfortable to those who have had limited experience with it. But over time nothing changed. He didn't send messages or calls on the hard days, like Father's Day and the date my dad passed away, which he was well aware of since I would constantly mention it as the day approached. When I asked why he didn't say anything to comfort me he responded with, "I don't know what to say." In a way he was right. There is nothing one can say that will take away the heartache of losing a loved one. But one can listen. The most significant, beneficial action to a grieving person is to reach out and let them know you are always there to listen. Even a hug during the darkest hours can make them a bit brighter. Although I had told him all the ways he could comfort me during difficult times, my boyfriend was not supportive of me and in fact I felt as if he distanced himself from me in the midst of them all. I know talking about grief isn't easy; for me it took years to talk about my dad without feeling pangs inside my chest. Still, because he was my boyfriend for such an extended period of time (almost four years) I had looked to him as a member of my support team, but I couldn't have been more wrong. Needless to say we are not together anymore, one of the reasons being he could not handle my past, which is a meaningful part of my present and future.

I was 13 when my dad passed away and always had my support system beside me, even when he was ill. When I began college, I no longer had my mother or sister to lean on when I needed an extra push to get through the day. I had trouble opening up to new people about my past and so not many of my new friends, even those I was closest to, knew that my dad was no longer with us. Phone calls to home helped but nothing compares to personal contact. I started experiencing anxiety from such unresolved feelings. I could not handle an unbalanced emotional state with the pressure of course work, especially without my family.

At the moment in time when I needed it the most, I found a peer-led support group for grieving students. I do not remember how or where I heard about the group, but it was just what I needed. I sat quietly during our first meeting, intimidated by the 20 or so students present. I had difficulty talking to my closest friends about my father, let alone a room full of strangers. But something happened at the end of the meeting that made me feel so at home and welcomed: hugs. Each member of the support group hugged one another. By the time I walked through the door to come home, I had received 20 hugs. It was unbelievable; I could not wait for the next meeting. A few tears fell and many laughs were had by the end of our discussion. I had never felt so comfortable yet vulnerable at the same time. Excitement and pride were all I could feel. Not only had I shared my story for the first time since my dad passed away but I didn't feel as if I was a burden. I felt empowered and stronger than ever before.

It was at the second meeting that I learned about a position to become more involved with the group and I applied and became the support group leader. It was through helping others that I began to heal. With each meeting I learned more about myself through learning about others. Meeting with students who "got it" gave me the courage to tell my story and I could not have done it without them.

Today, my heart still aches when I think of my dad and how much of my life he has missed and will miss out on. But today I am not intimidated to tell my story or talk about my feelings. I am eager to share my experience with others and hope that one day they will feel comfortable doing the same.

Questions for Reflection

Please reflect on and/or write out answers to the following questions:

1. In what ways, if any, were you able to connect with peers who had also experienced grief?

2. What were some of the feelings you experienced when you connected with a peer who had also experienced grief? Or what feelings have you experienced so far in reading this book?

3. If it was/has been challenging to identify and/or connect with grieving peers, what are some of the barriers you experienced?

4. What new ideas could you consider in finding and opening up to grieving peers?

5. If you have some concerns about others' perceptions or possible judgments, it would be helpful to consider in advance what you would like to share. How would you describe your loved one to someone who never met him or her? What stories would you share?

For supporters:

How can you help grieving college students or young adults to find a peer? Or how can you demonstrate that you also can provide the safe environment that they are looking for?

CHAPTER 5

Disconnection of Grief Expectations

Depending on a person's culture, there are often particular expectations and norms related to how one is "supposed" to grieve. These expectations are not always based on scientific research related to grief and they can leave grievers feeling like they are doing something wrong. Many of the authors addressed the differences they perceived between their experience with grief and the expectations of grief directly and indirectly communicated to them by others (e.g., friends, family members, society). Most specifically, students described their experience of grief as dynamic, complicated, unpredictable, and ongoing in contrast to messages that they received suggesting that grief has a timeline and moves in stages. One author compared grief to a "roller coaster" and another described it as coming in "waves." These expressions are in line with the most up-to-date research on grief: it is a process, does not move in predictable stages, in some ways never ends, and is unique for each person (Stroebe *et al.*, 2008).

The authors were sensitive to messages that implied judgment of their grief. One author noted that the expectations that she should "get over" her father's death became clear around six months, and that sympathy from others significantly declined around the same time. The authors perceived that the most supportive individuals listened to them with an open mind, acknowledged the complexity of their experience, and did not define them as people based on their bereavement status. It is possible that there can be even less sympathy for young adults who experience grief after they are out of college, because some people may perceive that grief is easier to cope with as you move further into adulthood.

Society's concept of "normal" grief is often inaccurate and grief can present in many different ways. It is important to note here that there is some controversy over a concept called "complicated" or "prolonged" grief, which some suggest requires specialized assistance (Shear and Shair, 2005). Researchers studying this concept argue that a small percentage (5–10%—and perhaps even lower for young adults) of grievers may develop a more intense and long-lasting form of grief that is marked by significant identity-related, work-related, and social difficulties for more than 12 months. People who may perceive themselves somehow "stuck" in their grief could possibly benefit from learning more about this concept (see Center for Complicated Grief, 2014). However, we do want to emphasize that we believe society has a limited definition of what "normal" grief is.

We have included the following two stories that we believe illustrate the importance of the grief expectations often experienced by grieving college students and young adults.

Katie

Sex: Female

Age: 22

Time since death loss: 1 year, 4 months

During college

Death loss: Brother

Drowned during seizure

I had just finished summer school and I was gearing up to fly off to school for a senior year of college filled with fun, nostalgia, and a slate of classes that I actually wanted to take. I'd had a rough year, but the last few months had at last been happy ones. After a great night of celebrating the end of my summer course and the start of a few weeks of vacation, I parted ways with my friends, eventually curling into bed and quickly falling peacefully and deeply asleep.

Six hours later my parents woke me up and were sitting on my bed. Before I could even realize how strange that was—considering they were supposed to be away—one of them spoke two words, telling me that my brother, my best friend, had died. I felt like I'd been stabbed, I started to wail, and I wanted more than I've ever wanted anything to be having one of those dreams where you think you've woken up but you're actually still dreaming. After more than a year, it's getting harder and harder to hope this isn't real. Some part of me will never stop hoping though; just as I hoped for a letter from Hogwarts at age 11, even when I was fairly convinced that the wizarding world could not be real.

As toddlers, my brother and I were so close in age and developmental stages that people used to think we were twins, but he was older than me and developed at a different pace because he was autistic. I had no idea what that meant as a toddler, nor do I think the doctors had settled on that description of him. In any case, I began to learn how to look out for him and accommodate his special needs at a very young age, and that was always a part of my life. First and foremost though, he was my brother. He had always been there as my partner in crime, an endless source of jokes, a source of annoyance (more than occasionally), and the frequent object of my peevish tricks. I would also use my playful side while trying to cheer him up or to steer him in the right direction, be it when he was anxious after having a seizure, overly obsessive to a problematic degree, or simply not able to take care of himself without a little direction. Although my parents, sister, and I had to work hard to help him, when the two of us were together, I felt more comfortable in my own skin than ever. Even when anything and everything else stressed me out, joking around with him was my best pick me up.

Although he had been epileptic since the middle of elementary school, his seizures were well controlled by medication. While it was a bit concerning when he had one, we always made sure someone's ears and eyes were on him and he took his meds on time. These aspects of our lives were so routine that his epilepsy was almost a non-issue. When he drowned due to a seizure in the water, it was the last thing I expected. He wasn't alone, but it happened quickly and even though watchful loving eyes were nearby and those present did all they could to save him, he was gone.

I honestly can't say why I hadn't thought more about the possibility, considering that he loved to swim, and would still be breathing but not able to control his body and stay afloat if he had a seizure. I could only envision my life with him in it, and the occasional times I had thought about his death, it was in the context of imagining how heartbroken I would be if as an elderly person he went before me. *How would I survive?* The thought that I would have to deal with it at the age of 20 had never crossed my mind. I suppose the one comfort is knowing that at least he did not know what hit him, and he was having a great day in good company at a spot our family treasured.

The time since then has often been incredibly difficult and painful. My grief affected and still affects all parts of my life. I can break down into tears at the sight of a favorite color, sound of a song, or any small detail that reminds me of my brother and how much I miss him.

For a long time, I could hardly tolerate being around people who were not good friends in social situations, because I had to decide what to share and make a choice between giving the true answer to most questions (e.g., So how's senior year? Looking forward to the holidays? What are your post-graduation plans? Want a drink? Having fun?) or to skirting around the truth. I felt awkward and unlike my typically open and expressive self.

As I tried to explain to my friends, everyone knows the feeling of how a very bad emotional day can leave you feeling very tired. In my grief, I had been having the worst days/hours/moments I'd ever had and many in a row for months. So even on a physical level I was totally wiped. Though I was usually able to sleep through the night, I used to (and sometimes still) wake up and feel physical and emotional pain, before I even knew why I was feeling it. A moment later I would remember that my brother died and it was like finding out all over again. Waking up can be horrible.

I've been disappointed that some people who love me cannot be there for me in ways that I would appreciate. Sometimes it is just too hard for them to deal with my grief, and sometimes they just don't know how to. That said, I've also been incredibly touched by the warmth of humanity, whether I encounter it in old friends and near strangers who reached out to our family, people who stopped me on the street to ask if I was all right when I was upset, friends who have supported me in the best ways they know how, and all kinds of people who accepted it when I poured my heart out and responded as honestly as they could.

It is odd to be grateful for these experiences as I wouldn't wish them on anyone. I am grateful though, as my grief has better equipped me to be there for people going through rough times. It has reinforced my feeling that in many cases no one can know what you are going through, but that doesn't mean all hope is lost. I think that for many people, when someone they care for is in distress, they want to have answers for them and think they can be an anchor that calms their turbulence. To say that you do *not* fully know how they feel or what they should do may seem like a scary uncertain thing to say, but, at least for me, hearing that kind of honesty can be liberating. I feel much more comfortable with people who may not "get it," but can acknowledge that they don't. While they mean well, those who don't acknowledge their ignorance end up frustrating and isolating me with pep talks, explanations, and "solutions."

I think that no one will fully "get it" because they are not living my life, and my relationship with my brother was/is unlike any other. We were siblings, quite close, but not in the usual way of confiding in one another and bonding over deep conversation. I helped take care of him, and would have had to take on more caregiver responsibilities over the years, had he not died. My experience grieving for him is just as unique as our relationship was.

Though in your twenties a year and a half may seem like forever, my brother's death is still a new reality. Grieving for him, and my life with him in it, has shaped my time since then. I'm sure it will continue to shape my future. Actually, the way I thought about the future changed. While my peers were freaking out about how "old" we were as we finished up undergrad and worried that they still didn't know what they were doing, I was focused on how my brother died at an incredibly young age. In all likelihood our own deaths would not be soon, and it was OK if I took my sweet time to figure out what I wanted to do with myself. I took breaks when I needed them, and still do. I completely changed my plan for the time after graduation, and I'm convinced I'm much better off for it.

I dislike it when people encourage me to move on, or suggest that such a thing will happen soon. Though it may sound depressing to some, I have no interest in "moving on." That would mean pushing the first chapters of my life aside, pretending this loss is not a permanent scar, and that my love for my brother would be less a part of my life than ever before. Even the thought of that terrifies me. My memories are already fading bit by bit (which I hate), but I know that despite that, my bond with my brother will never weaken. For me it is actually comforting to know that the ups and downs of remembering and missing him will always be a part of me. I do not want my love for him to diminish, nor do I think it even could, and as long as I love him I'll miss him. My grief changes and I don't always know what's coming, but I do not believe those who say it will get better every day. I think that the only certain thing about it is that it will remain and evolve.

Despite these challenges, I have managed. Of that, I am proud. My priority has always been taking care of myself and, for me, that includes letting myself feel whatever I'm feeling. Right now, I no longer cry every day and I can much better handle spending time in large social situations, but my grief shows itself in different ways that are less visible to my friends. People have commented sometimes that I seem "better," which makes it sounds like they think this is like having the flu. They do not appreciate how grief is complex and multifaceted, and it will always be with me, even when my living and breathing brother can't be.

Samantha

Sex: Female

Age: 21

Time since death loss:
10 years

Prior to college

Death loss: Father

Septic shock after gastric
bypass surgery

You could say that my "story" began seven-and-a-half years before I began my first year of college.

Throughout my childhood, my dad, who was morbidly obese, struggled with his weight. Buzzwords included "exercise," "dieting," "Weight Watchers," "Atkins," and on and on and on.

Ultimately, on Monday, November 25, 2002, he elected to undergo gastric bypass surgery. Though there are inherent risks with any surgery, those for this particular procedure were downplayed. At the time, we were told that only 0.5 percent of patients experienced complications from the surgery, a statistic that has not held up over the years. One in 200? Not terrible odds. We weren't particularly worried.

Two days later—though he protested because he felt something wasn't quite right—my dad was discharged from the hospital. The following morning, my two-year-old brother, my eight-year-old sister and my 11-year-old self bounded down the stairs, ready to watch the Macy's Thanksgiving Day Parade. Almost immediately, a frantic version of my mother ushered us back upstairs, instructing me to keep my sister and brother occupied until further notice.

As the day progressed, I would periodically tiptoe to the top of the stairs, eavesdropping on what was unfolding below. I heard my dad moaning in pain, and I heard my mom on the phone with his doctor insisting that something was wrong and begging for him to meet us at the hospital.

Around 1pm, I met my mom in the upstairs hallway to find her packing a bag for me and my siblings. She guided us to the car where my dad was waiting in the passenger seat. She began the two-minute drive to a neighbor's house. Each of the four turns along the way caused my dad what had to have been excruciating pain, as the last words I ever heard him say—aside from a strained and nearly inaudible "love you"—were, "Easy, Lisa. Easy."

The next two days consisted of various adults telling us his doctor had figured out what was wrong with my dad. He'd be home soon and though my mom was too busy to call, everything was fine. But on Saturday, mid-Christmas movie, as my siblings and I sat on the couch of yet another family friend, the phone was passed to me. On the other end of the line was my mother, crying. She managed to get out, "Daddy's in surgery now, and he's probably going to die. Even if he makes it, there's still a really good chance that he'll die. Donna's going to bring you to the hospital now."

Cue the tears, and cue the shock.

Less than one hour later, my sister and I entered the hospital elevator. As I watched Donna press the button for the Intensive Care Unit, I pointed to the nearby sign indicating that children under age 13 were not permitted on the floor. "I know," she said. "You're fine."

Walking into the waiting room, we were immediately greeted with forced smiles from nearly all of my extended family.

What? Uncles and aunts from across the nation whom I had not seen for at least a year all knew before us?

A few hours later, my dad's doctor stood in the doorway delivering the good news that my dad was out of surgery. It had gone as well as it could have, yet our collective sigh of relief was interrupted by the doctor's wary warning: "We're not out of the dark yet."

Later that evening, we all begrudgingly left the hospital. I vividly remember lying in bed hoping, wishing, and praying harder than ever before in my life.

Please just let him live.

At 6:52am the next morning, Donna shook my sister and I awake. The urgency in her voice was palpable, and strawberry Pop-tarts were tossed to us as we climbed into the backseat of her van.

We would later found out that we entered the hospital the very minute my dad died. His stomach had not been sealed correctly during his initial surgery. The discovery of this came too late, ultimately causing his body to go into septic shock. His kidneys failed, he experienced numerous heart attacks and at 7:42am on Sunday, December 1, 2002, he died.

At 11 years old, I had been the textbook example of a "daddy's girl," and the following months were incredibly difficult. Not only did I feel different from my "normal" peers, but I also felt detached from my own family. Simply put, I felt completely alone.

There were those who I truly believe—years later (hindsight is 20/20 after all)—meant well, despite my frustration with them at the time. It wasn't necessarily that they said or did the "wrong" thing. It's that I was angry. I was angry after my dad died. I was angry he was gone, jealous my friends still had their "perfect" lives and annoyed with those whom I believed were pretending to understand. I often reacted negatively to genuine, well-meaning comments because grief and the emotions that come with grief dominated my thoughts.

Thankfully, six months later, I found a community of people who got it at Comfort Zone Camp, the United States' largest free bereavement camp for children who have experienced the death of a parent, sibling, or primary caregiver. Sharing my story and simply talking in a supportive environment taught me how to cope positively with my grief. It let me find the good amidst the bad. And, it helped me learn to grieve the memories I had yet to make with my dad, the memories I felt I had been robbed of.

The next seven years consisted of a series of milestones and changes—all without my dad. Graduating elementary school.

School plays, band concerts, piano recitals, and swim meets. Watching my mom begin to date. Father–daughter dances. My little brother starting school. Moving to a new house with my mom's boyfriend and his daughter. Graduating middle school. Family vacations. Changing high schools. Report cards. Jobs. A myriad of accomplishments. College applications. Boyfriends. Graduating high school. And countless other moments.

Then, seven years, eight months and 20 days after my dad died, I found myself moving into my dorm at UNC-Chapel Hill, ready to begin my first year. As my mom and her longtime boyfriend of six years helped me loft my bed, small thoughts that I hadn't had in years crept into my mind—the this-isn't-how-its-supposed-to-be-thoughts.

This isn't how it's supposed to be. He's supposed to be here. My dad is supposed to be here keeping my mom calm and using the latest piece of technology (an iPhone, no doubt) to check off our day's accomplishments on his slightly obsessive packing and to-do lists.

Fast-forward to October 17, what would have been my dad's 52nd birthday. It was my first time experiencing a "Dad day" without my family. To say it hit me harder than the past few years' worth of birthdays combined would be an understatement.

The next month was the eighth anniversary of his death. My suite mates weren't exactly sure what to do when they found me curled up in my room that evening looking at pictures, listening to Luther Vandross' "Dance with My Father," Eric Clapton's "Tears in Heaven," *West Side Story*'s "Somewhere," and Bob Carlisle's "Butterfly Kisses" and surrounded by a box's worth of wadded up tissues.

Eight years later and still having days when I'm this upset and in hysterics? Yup.

I am a staunch believer that grief is not something that ever goes away. Yes it changes, and yes it becomes less consuming. But does it ever go away? Definitely not. College reaffirmed this for me. Being in a new environment without my family and the support of friends from home was initially isolating. My first semester was especially difficult.

I do not want to downplay how amazingly supportive the people in my life are. However, there are some interesting things about grieving an "old loss" within the college bubble.

First, there's the simple and unfortunate fact that time is/ was working against me. For some reason, society has placed an arbitrary expiration date on grief. I began to notice the decline in sympathy and understanding six to 12 months following my dad's death, and as time passed further, the expectation that I'd "get over it" increased as well. Because of this, it came as no surprise when my college peers were thrown off when I had bad days—after all, my loss was ten years ago.

You see, those who have never experienced an immediate loss—through no fault of their own—often buy into the you-get-over-it myth. Perhaps it's because they hope that if they lost a loved one, they'd only face that unimaginable pain for a short amount of time. But when you're surrounded by people who can't understand that grief comes in waves—that years later, you may be reduced to tears from simply seeing a girl carried on her father's shoulders at the football game—you can start to feel as if there's something wrong with you, as if you are grieving the "wrong way."

Second, the fast-paced environment that is college isn't particularly conducive to grieving. Between classes, deadlines, extracurricular activities, meals, studying, parties, events, and trying to squeeze in some sleep, there isn't much wiggle room for adding in reflection or bad days to your schedule. And, when you factor in the expectation that you should always be on the go or ready to have a good time (these are supposed to be "the best days of your life," right?), grief can become a burden.

And finally, there are the times when I'm sharing a memory and realize the person with whom I'm speaking just isn't getting it. They never knew my dad, so they're having a hard time picturing this almost-mythical figure I'm gushing about. For them, he's simply a collection of fragmented stories—memories of a little girl. How can I even come close to adequately describing him? There are days when it absolutely crushes me to remember the truth: I can't. People are so much more than their occupations, their likes and dislikes or their talents. It's about the moments you shared with them. How they could draw people in. How their presence could fill a room. The unconditional love. The pride. The laughs. The corny jokes. The embraces. It's all of the intangible things you can't put your finger on. It's the life that made that person special. It's how having that person in your life made you feel. The majority of the people now in my life never knew my dad. I wish they could have. Maybe then, it would be easier for them to grasp what I'm missing.

It's been ten years since my dad's death and most days I'm happy. Really, most around me would never know I still grieve. They don't experience the memories that are triggered daily. They aren't privy to my thoughts when the what-would-life-be-like questions begin to play through my head. Now, it seems that most people only recognize my grief if I broadcast that it's there. For example, on my dad's birthday, my Facebook profile picture changes to one of us together. I do it for myself because there's something in me that needs to be able to wave my hands as if to say, "Hey world, I still miss him! Thousands of days have passed, but I still grieve and it still hurts." It's ironic in a way. After he first died, I hated feeling like I was "the girl whose Dad died." But now? I just want people to remember him, even if it's for just one day of the year. I want people to remember that his death changed me.

I accepted my new normal years ago and learned to love my life and live it for what it is. His death is no longer one of the first things I remind myself of when I wake up, nor is it the last thing I think about before I fall asleep; it no longer consumes me. Yet, there are still days when I break down crying, and there are times when I want to scream about how unfair it all is; these days are normal for me. Being used to something doesn't mean it's always easy. And those who love me understand—to the best of their ability—that these days will forever be a part of who I am.

Questions for Reflection

Please reflect on and/or write out answers to the following questions:

1. Prior to your own grief experiences, what were some of the expectations (e.g., length of time, difficulty) that you had about grief?

2. What expectations (e.g., that you would drop out, have others to turn to, grades would change), if any, did you have about how your grief would affect you during college?

3. How was your grief similar, and different, to what you may have expected?

For supporters:

> What were/have been some of the expectations you have about the grief of the college student(s) and/or young adult(s) you seek to support (e.g., length of time, difficulty)? How has their grief been similar and different from what you expected? What could you have done differently, or still do differently, to let these young people know that you understand grief is unique to each person?

CHAPTER 6

Life Transition Challenges

Life transitions can present new challenges for grievers. For young adults, major life transitions may include starting and graduating from college, beginning a career, establishing a relationship with a life partner, and having children (Arnett, 2004). Our authors described these transitions as periods of heightened reflection, reaction, and interpersonal negotiation. Not surprisingly, sadness was often associated with these transitions. Students who had experienced their death loss during childhood or early adolescence indicated significant internal struggle as they began college, particularly related to whether or not to be honest and open with peers about their grief. A few specifically noted that they intentionally decided to be vague or even lie in order to avoid discomfort on the part of their peers.

Those who experienced a death loss during college shared about the difficult transition of returning to school and the lack of acknowledgement of their loss and the challenge of returning to a setting that was continuing on as normal. For the authors whose loved ones were ill while they were in college, there were stresses, strains, and sometimes conflicts related to their frequent transitions from home to school and back again. They sometimes reported living in two worlds and never feeling like they were in the "right" place.

Other authors viewed graduation as a marking point related to their grief in the context of their deceased loved one being absent and to entering a work setting where decisions have to be made regarding disclosure of their death loss experience. Thoughts about future life transitions, such as marriage and childbirth also presented challenges for several authors.

We have included the following three stories that we believe highlight the life transition challenges often faced by grieving college students and young adults.

Sarah

Sex: Female

Age: 23

Time since death loss:
2 years, 8 months

During college

Death loss: Mother

Breast cancer

I am about to enter into a new phase of my life, a phase where I must learn to be on my own, in more ways than one. I am graduating from college.

Although I'm extremely excited about what the future holds for me, I am sad that I am saying goodbye. For me, saying goodbye means that my college experience is truly ending; and that's incredibly scary for me. I feel like, in a way, I'm once again going to have to say goodbye to my mom and try to move on in my life without her. My mom passed away during my first year at Meredith College. Her death is the most defining moment of my life, thus far. I love my mother more than anyone will ever be able to know or understand. She was, and still is, the most important and influential person in my life.

My mom was diagnosed with breast cancer when I was a freshman in high school. I can still recall sitting on my parents' bed looking down at the bedspread as my mother spoke the three words that would change my life from that moment on: "I have cancer." At first, I didn't truly understand how serious her diagnosis was. Looking back, I realize that my mother tried to shield me and my sister from the seriousness of her condition.

I remember sitting beside her in the hair salon as the hair stylist shaved what little hair was left, after she had begun chemotherapy.

I cried, while my mother looked at me and said, "It's just hair. It will grow back, and I will be OK." Even before her surgical procedures, she would tell me, "Sarah, I'm going to be fine. Don't worry about me." I remember standing beside the bathroom door, as she crouched in front of the toilet, violently ill, thanks to the chemo. Over time, I began to accept that my mother having cancer was my new "normal." For me, hearing about my mom's chemo and radiation treatments was about as routine as hearing about my sister's day at school.

It was during my senior year of high school when things began to change. It was during that year that my family and I discovered that my mother's cancer had spread to her brain. Like she had done so many times before, my mother tried to reassure us that she was going to be fine. And just like I had done a few years before, I began to accept my mother's new condition as the new "normal." Pretty soon after the diagnosis, I became focused on applying to colleges. In some ways, the distraction was welcome.

Freshman year of college came, and I was focused on attending classes, trying to determine what I wanted to do for the rest of my life. The year soon flew by and before I knew it, I was at home for the summer.

In July, we discovered that my mother's brain tumor was back with a vengeance. The following month, my mother went in for surgery to remove the fast-growing tumor. A couple of weeks later, I returned to college, to begin my sophomore year. Secretly, I had been dreading the thought of going back. I thought that if I went back to school, perhaps studying and spending time with friends would help. What I realized was that I was severely unhappy. Three weeks into my fall semester, I decided to take time off from school. For many, it seemed as though I made that decision on the spur of the moment. Perhaps I did, but I felt it was the right thing for me to do.

That December we discovered that the tumor was back. The physicians told my mother that she had one last option, to try and eradicate the tumor: whole brain radiation. In the bluntest of terms, my mom's brain was going to be fried in the hopes that the tumor would die quickly. I sometimes wonder, if I had been in her place, what would I have done? Would I have made the decision like she did, to risk losing a part of myself, in the hopes of living longer? Or, would I have said, "No. I want to enjoy the time I have left." I don't know what my decision would have been, but I do know that my mom made her decision with the best of intentions.

I remember the night before she had her first round of radiation. We were standing in our kitchen; she looked at me and said, "Is there anything you want me to tell you about anything at all, in case I forget after tomorrow?" There were so many things that I wanted to ask her, but didn't. So I asked if she could sing me my favorite song, from when I was a kid: "The Walking Song" by Raffi. She sang the chorus, but couldn't remember the rest. Thinking about her singing that song, still brings a smile to my face.

Sadly, that's the last memory I have of my mom of when she was really "my mom." The radiation treatments altered her brain, to the point where I felt like my mother had died and an alien had invaded her body. Growing up, my mother had always been patient, willing to listen and offer advice whenever someone needed it, and had a wicked sense of humor. That woman left, the woman who took her place was very impatient with her mood always changing. In some ways, she was almost psychotic. The rational side to her brain simply disappeared. There were days I was afraid to be around her.

In August, I started at a new college, Meredith College. I was excited to be going back to a college campus and to be feeling like a college student again. What I didn't realize was that the transition back to being a college student would be difficult. The first few months were lonely. I didn't really know anyone at the school and it was hard to talk about my mom and what my family was going through. If I did ever share that my mom was sick, I would usually get the pursed lips and the "oh" reaction. What had been a friendly conversation quickly turned into an uncomfortable one.

In October 2009, we were told there was nothing more that could be done to treat my mom's cancer. My mother was given an official timeline of six months. At that point, I was almost relieved that a timeline had been given. For me, it meant that although I was losing my mom, having to deal with cancer and the horrible situation involved with it, was almost done. We—my mom, dad, sister, and myself—were all tired of it. Cancer doesn't just affect the person with the disease, it affects everyone they are in contact with. I may have not fought the disease in the physical sense, but I fought it emotionally and mentally.

October was also the month that I discovered a support group for college students who were dealing with the illness or loss of a loved one. I debated back and forth about whether I should try it or not. I was afraid of opening up to a bunch of strangers about what was going on. I was scared that they were going to judge me for what I thought or felt. Despite all my fears, this tiny voice in my head kept saying, "Try it. If you don't like it, you don't ever have to go back." Strangely, that voice sounded a lot like my mom. Walking to that first support group, was one of the most difficult walks in my life, but when it was my turn, I started to speak, and almost immediately wanted to cry. Everyone just sat and listened; no one judged me for what I was feeling. No one said what I was feeling was wrong. They got it. As I walked out of the room after the session had ended I felt relief. It was as though a boulder had been removed from my shoulders, and for the first time in a long time, I actually felt like I was going to be OK. Over the course of the next few months, support group gradually changed from something that I was trying, into something that I desperately needed. Support group became my rock.

January soon turned into February, and February into March. Over the course of those three months, my mom's illness grew worse. I would call home every day and every day my dad would either say, "She's sleeping," or, "She'll probably only talk to you for a few minutes." Either answer was fine with me, because it meant that she was still alive.

When I arrived home for Spring Break, my mom opened the door to the house before I could even knock. She smiled at me and said in a cheery voice, "Welcome home!" I hugged her and walked into the house. After setting my bags on the floor, my dad announced that dinner was ready. As we began to eat, my mom looked at my dad and asked, "When are Sarah and Elizabeth coming home?" My dad smiled at her and said, "Well Sarah's right here. She just arrived about ten minutes ago." My mom turned and looked at me, before saying, "Oh, of course. Silly me." At that point, I knew my mom didn't have much time left. Four days later, my mom decided to take a nap. When she woke up, she was no longer able to sit up. One week later, she was gone.

The night she passed away, I was sitting in the room with her, holding her hand. I had only arrived about 20 minutes beforehand, having gone to grab a quick bite to eat. Walking into the room, the only sound I could hear was her breathing, labored and gasping. I walked over to the chair beside her bed and sat down. Grabbing her hand, I began to rub it with my thumb. With tears streaming down my face, I kept repeating, "Mom, Dad, Elizabeth, and I are so proud of you. We love you, and we're going to be OK. We're going to be OK." Eventually, I forced myself to say, "It's OK to let go." I hesitated in saying those words, because saying them meant that this was my final goodbye to her. A few minutes later the room became quiet. My dad walked in almost immediately after and we just stood and hugged.

Three days after my mom passed away, I returned to college. I wanted to feel normal again. I craved structure, and stability. The next few months following my mother's death were the some of the darkest days of my life. I would wake up always in a haze. I was numb. I didn't feel anything and didn't want to do anything. I would just sit in my room. When I wasn't numb, I was angry. Unfortunately, my family got the brunt of my anger. I would cry and yell. I couldn't explain why I was angry, I just was. At one point, I yelled at my dad, "Why can't you step up and be a better parent?!" I know I hurt him deeply when I said that. It's not something I'm proud of and I wish I could take it back.

In terms of school, I went to class and for the most part tried to pay attention to what was being taught. I was extremely fortunate to have had professors who understood, and cared about what I was going through. I even had one professor say, "If you don't want to come to class, you don't need to. We can figure out your assignments, later." There were some days that I just didn't want to get out bed. Other days, I almost felt normal again. But I got through the semester.

The first year without my mom was difficult. There were days, when all I wished for was to hear her voice again. Little by little, I began to feel "normal" again.

The idea that there are five stages of grief is absurd. You don't graduate from one stage to the next. Rather, grief becomes a part of your life almost like a chronic condition. You'll have good days and you'll have bad ones. Embrace the good with the bad. What I have taken away from my experience, more than anything, is the knowledge that I know more about myself than I ever have before. I miss my mom more than anything in the world, but I wouldn't change the experience that I've had. Her death, as well as her life, taught me valuable life lessons, and I am forever grateful for them.

I am going to be OK.

Kate

Sex: Female

Age: 27

Time since death loss:
12 years, 4 months and
11 years, 9 months

Prior to college

Death loss: Sister and mother

Neuroblastoma (sister),
glioblastoma (mother)

When I was five years old and my sister Courtney was three, she was diagnosed with neuroblastoma, a type of solid tumor that, in her case, had already spread all over her body before they even diagnosed it.

The following ten years, my family traveled the country in search of the next treatment that could help cure or ultimately just try to control this relentless cancer. Weeks in the hospital and late-night fevers with trips to the emergency room became a normal part of our lives. Vacations were canceled and Christmas mornings were spent in the hospital. But through it all, my parents did an extraordinary job of showing us how to love and support each other, to persevere through the toughest challenges, and to sincerely value life and the people around you. My parents truly are the two most amazing people I have ever had in my life for more reasons than I can mention here. They have made me into the person I am today, and they have shaped how I live my life. Sadly, we lost my little sister to her battle with neuroblastoma in September 2000, when she was 13 years old and her ferocious little heart had given all that it could.

I was a sophomore in high school when Courtney passed away. My support system at that time consisted of my parents, my other siblings, my extended family, and a large community of friends from both our grade school and high school. Our family felt completely embraced by the hundreds of people who wanted to help.

About a month after my sister passed away, my mom started having headaches and was feeling more tired than usual. We first chalked it up to stress related to the loss of my sister, but when she also started having vision changes my dad took her to the doctor. My mom was diagnosed with a glioblastoma, a highly malignant brain tumor. Are. You. Kidding. Me?

The six months from October 2000 to April 2001 were just a blur. My mom passed away in what seemed like a blink of an eye. I don't know that any more sorrow or grief could come out of one year. Again, my dad, siblings, extended family, and community of friends came out to support me. Living at home with them and having the same routine of school and extracurriculars helped ease the coping process. Everyone I interacted with knew my family's story. They were sensitive to what I had been through, and even if they didn't say anything specific, I knew that they had some understanding of what I was dealing with. That was not at all true when I went away to college.

I started my freshman year at Georgetown University in the fall of 2003, just over two years after losing my mom and sister. Nobody there knew my story, nobody there even suspected to ask. Not many kids had lost a family member, let alone a sister and a mother when they were 16 years old. College marked a fresh start where I could try to move on from all of the sadness I had been dealing with for the past few years. I thought that would be good for me, and I figured the anonymity would help me to form my own identity outside of being a part of the family who had suffered great loss.

What I was surprised to discover was that I missed people knowing my story, because that meant that I didn't have to tell them. Now I was faced with having to first tell my entire story before I could share a thought or a feeling that related to my mom or sister. This was a greater task than I had realized. I found myself keeping a lot of those thoughts to myself because it was easier than having to explain my family history. I missed people asking how my family and I were doing. Even though I knew it was because they didn't know, it still felt like it was because they didn't care. It was hard to exchange life stories with new friends, knowing that a huge part of my life was missing. Birthdays and anniversaries of passings were near impossible to observe without letting too much emotion show. Worst of all, I couldn't help but feel that I was doing a poor job of honoring my mom's and sister's memories.

That situation changed for me one night when my roommate and I went out with a couple of the football guys we had become friends with. We were walking through campus, when one friend mentioned something about his mom who had been diagnosed with a brain tumor. Something instantly clicked inside of me—someone else who might actually have some idea about what I had been going through. I felt a sense of sadness and devastation for my friend and his family. But at the same time, I also felt empathy, compassion, and even a sense of relief, because, besides my siblings, I had never met anyone else who could truly understand what that felt like. After my friend lost his mother, he started a support group for kids who were dealing with sickness or death in their family. I attended the very first meeting, not knowing what to expect and, as kids started trickling in, sharing their stories and opening up about their sorrows and triumphs over dealing with a sick or passed loved one, warmth came to my heart because I knew my friend had started something great. Being able to openly discuss our experiences, and receptively listen to others' as well, became truly therapeutic. I did not feel judged or pitied. Above all, my silence had been broken. I no longer had to keep my loss to myself. I realized that many people in my current and future life may never know about my mom and sister, but now there was a group who would. And that was a great start to unlocking the mystery of dealing with my grief in this new stage of my life.

As time went on and I became more comfortable with my college friends, talking about my mom and sister became easier. Just being able to express certain thoughts and feelings helped me tremendously in the healing process. A few close friends became confidants who were always available to listen and talk. These people were an invaluable support. I went to late-night Mass by myself, not so much to pray, but more so to have quiet time to sit and talk to my mom. I found that dealing with the loss of my mom was harder than dealing with the loss of my sister. I had grown up with my sister being sick, so subconsciously I think I always knew that death may be a possibility. However, I had never expected to lose my mom when and how I did. The brief illness and seemingly sudden death was harder to understand and accept. I did a lot of thinking, and crying, and drinking in college. I had always prided myself on being emotionally tough, but being alone away from home and faced with such grief proved to be harder than I had imagined. Ultimately, I think it was a combination of time, my family, close friends, and a lot of reflective thinking that guided me through my grief.

Having said that, if I had to single out one person who helped me the most, it would hands down be my dad. He provided us with unwavering love and support. His example of emotional strength and resilience was incredible. He had lost his life partner and his youngest daughter, yet he somehow maintained a positive outlook on life. He put our new lives into perspective for us, and he was the rock that anchored us together. Whenever I was struggling with my thoughts or emotions, I would call my dad to talk it out with him. His advice was always so simple, yet wise. He taught me that it was my decision as to how I would let this grief affect my life. I could not change how I felt, but I could make some effort to guide how those feelings impacted the way I lived my life. I could let the sorrow overwhelm me, or I could reach out and try to live my life to the fullest despite my loss. This was an important realization for me, because for a long time, I felt that there was nothing I could do about feeling horrible, lost, and angry. I learned to process my feelings in a different way. I eventually was able to accept certain emotions, while simultaneously analyzing what they meant to me and evaluating what role they would play in my life. It is a challenge, even to this day, but it is a mental and emotional framework that allows me to embrace my grief and cope with it to the best of my ability.

When I was a kid, I never would have imagined that my life would unfold as it did. However, even if I had, I do not believe there would have been any way to adequately prepare. There is no universal handbook on grief and loss, as everyone's experience with it is so unique. I was lucky enough to find the support and guidance that I needed in order to make it through the toughest times. It has been over a decade since I lost my mom and sister, and while there will always be some degree of sorrow that is tied to their loss, I have come to understand that life is an evolution. My mom and sister may not be here to physically witness my life today, but I know they would be proud to see what I am doing today as a pediatric oncology nurse. My mom may not be able to attend my wedding or become a grandmother, but she taught me how to unconditionally love and how to strive to be the most amazing parent.

My life will never be the same without my mom and sister, but I hold them and all they have taught me in the center of my heart. They are with me even though they are not physically with me. I believe that where something is lost, something can always be gained. In my case, my grief taught me about myself, my love and appreciation for my family and friends, my passion for nursing, and the bittersweet importance of embracing both the sorrows and joys of life to the fullest.

Julie

Sex: Female

Age: 26

Time since death loss:
3 years, 7 months

Sick prior and died soon after college

Death loss: Father

Amyotrophic lateral sclerosis

During my senior year in high school, I started to notice that my dad was having trouble using his hands. He stopped playing golf, using a fork and knife became difficult, and gripping the steering wheel was a challenge for him. In the summer of 2005, shortly before I left for college, my parents sat down with me, my brother, and my sister and told us that Dad had a neurological disorder that would cause him to become paralyzed. They emphasized, however, that he would not die, and promised that he would be there to see me graduate from college. I remember feeling numb, just wanting to get away from the table where we sat. Mom was crying and I stormed off to take a shower. A few minutes after the water hit me, so did the meaning of what I had been told. I was uncertain about whether I should leave in August, but Dad insisted that I still go to Georgetown for college, even though it was a four-hour drive from my home in Pittsburgh.

When I arrived at college, I managed to pretend nothing was wrong for about a month. During freshman move-in weekend, my family and I heard a student talk about a peer support group for students with ill parents or those whose parents had died. I did not think it applied to me since my dad was not dying, and I just wanted to try to ignore his illness as much as possible. My ability to pretend that something terrible was not happening to my family came to an end in late September of my freshman year. My mom called me crying and asked me to come home for my dad's birthday the next weekend. I resisted, arguing that I was trying to make friends and settle in at college. Finally my mom broke down and told me the truth: my dad had amyotrophic lateral sclerosis (ALS), a fatal neurological illness that has no cure. They had lied about the extent of his illness in order to protect me and my siblings from the truth for as long as possible. This revelation knocked the wind out of me. It was so final, so horribly inevitable.

In light of this discovery, I offered to move home and go to a local college. I felt I should go home not only so that I could spend as much time as possible with my dad, but also because I felt guilty—and continued to feel guilty throughout my time at Georgetown—for being the one member of my family who was not helping out with my dad's care; the one member whose schedule was not dictated by my dad's needs and who could, once in a while, even forget he was sick. My dad was extremely adamant, however, that I stay at Georgetown. He insisted that he wanted me to continue to have as normal a life as possible, despite his illness.

Life felt anything but normal. When I found out that my dad was dying, I had known my new friends for all of six weeks. Although I told my roommate and a few closer friends at Georgetown, none of them had lost a parent and they seemed sympathetic but unsure of what to say. I also did not know what to say, or how much I could talk about feeling sad or worried before my friends would abandon me for being so depressing and needy. So I pretended to be fine and avoided talking about my dad's illness with my college friends. I felt utterly alone, and was convinced that no one had ever gone through what I was experiencing. Then my mom reminded me of the student who had talked about the support group during orientation.

At the first support group meeting, I felt a great sense of relief. There were other people at school who were going through the same thing or had gone through it and had come out on the other side relatively intact. Listening to the others talk, I found that my feelings and experiences were not entirely unique, and I took comfort in that. I also got to tell my story and not feel that I was imposing on anyone—we were all there both to give and receive support. As I returned to more meetings, I became friends with a couple of the support group members and we reached out to each other outside of the support group when we were having trouble getting through the day.

I began going home for about one weekend per month. These trips were both precious and devastating. They always began with an initial shock—my dad had gone from using a cane to a walker, or a walker to a wheelchair, but no one had told me because they did not want to upset me. There was also the shock of seeing my dad in a more deteriorated condition—weaker, having more difficulty speaking, becoming more frustrated daily with his physical limitations. The house itself was a different place. We had an elevator installed, there was a ramp to the front door, and, eventually, there were caretakers tending to my dad.

My family members changed. My sister, who turned 15 shortly after I left for college and had a history of depression, started experimenting with drugs and sex, becoming secretive and losing weight rapidly, all of which were part of her first full-blown manic episode—a condition that would culminate in a suicide attempt and a diagnosis of bipolar disorder during the summer after my freshman year. My brother, who was 17, started skipping class to smoke weed, and would disappear for days at a time without a word. He would eventually drop out of high school and was in rehab on the night that my sister first attempted suicide. My brother and I had been very close, but all of a sudden he was sneaking around or completely absent. It was as if each sibling had gone to his or her separate corner to deal with the fallout of my dad's illness.

My mom, on the other hand, was in survival mode. This meant that she was trying to keep my brother in school, manage my sister's illness, and care for Dad. When I came home to visit, she would sometimes drop an off-hand remark about the fact that I was not home to help and expected me to do a lot of chores and caretaking to lift the burden from her a bit. This fueled my pre-existing guilt. I was the highest-functioning family member, the only one she was not caring for, so I was her greatest source of help. I would come to resent her for seeing me in this light, even though now I can see she was just desperate to keep everyone afloat.

Spending time with my dad was painful in some ways, but also reassuring and comforting in others. To spend time with Dad meant also to care for him, whether it was getting him water or adjusting his position or changing the channel or giving him medicine. At first I felt very shy about caring for my dad. I felt his embarrassment at his inability to care for himself as he slowly lost control of his own body. His frustration, especially at the beginning, both frightened and saddened me. Still, we eventually established a rhythm, one that adjusted over time to accommodate his increasing needs. Once we found that, we were able to watch movies together and have some conversations, the memory of which I cherish to this day.

Returning to Georgetown for sophomore year was frightening but also a relief. I was scared to get into the same pattern of feeling guilty for not being at home and experiencing shock and terrible sadness whenever I visited my family, but I was also relieved to get away from my sad, damaged family and be able to continue to create a life independent from them. I wanted a life that was free of sadness, illness, and death. I wanted a separate existence at school that did not include everything horrible that was happening at home. Obviously, this was impossible and the strongest indication of that fact was probably my daily panic attacks. I started seeing a therapist at school and eventually took medicine to help with my anxiety. A lot of my anxiety had to do with being afraid of feeling sad. Not just the sadness that was always there, but those horrible rushes of overwhelming pain and crushing hopelessness that took my breath away.

Even more frightening was expressing sadness in front of other people. Whenever my mom cried, I felt myself shut down emotionally. I was angry at her for crying—for being weak, as I saw it, when I needed to rely on someone. The same thing happened with my friends. I would share something that had happened to my dad recently, or perhaps I would tell a new friend about his illness, and she would cry and I would feel utterly numb. I felt like there was something wrong with me. The only place this did not happen was at the support group meetings. There, I did not feel self-conscious about crying. Often, however, I would cry when the other group members were telling their own stories. I know I was crying for myself and my family as well, but it was easier to let it out if someone else was doing the talking.

I also engaged in service activities. Working on projects made me feel that, even though I could not control my father's illness or the chaos at home, I could be proactive in some way. Attending the Walk to Defeat ALS each fall was particularly important to me. It allowed me to feel as if I were helping my dad and others who were going through the same thing by raising money and awareness. It also provided a means of bringing up the fact of my dad's illness to my friends and allowing them to support me by attending the event, rather than the more uncomfortable option of talking about my feelings with them.

Many of my friends went abroad during my junior year in college. This was difficult not only because I lost them as sources of support and companionship, but also because I felt limited by my dad's illness. Throughout college I experienced intermittent periods of frustration at the feeling of being held back by my dad's illness and the complicated circumstances of my family. I felt this on a small scale when I missed an event like a basketball game or a close friend's birthday party because I was going home for the weekend. I felt it on a larger scale when my friends got summer internships in other cities and studied abroad, whereas I spent each summer at home and did not go abroad for fear of being far away if something happened to my dad. These feelings of jealousy and frustration were always accompanied by intense guilt for having felt them in the first place. I was ashamed of not wanting to go home on a particular weekend or wishing I could go abroad when I knew these were my last years with my dad.

My dad's condition worsened almost without interruption during my four years at college, so I felt as if I were losing him little by little. I grieved the loss of his ability to walk, then to speak, then to swallow food. It felt like a constant grieving process coupled with a terrible fear of his eventual death. As the end neared, I shut down more and more. During my senior year, I spoke less about my feelings to my friends, family, and boyfriend, and tried to avoid discussing the most difficult feelings with my therapist. My anxiety and depression became more acute, and I found myself spending a lot of time alone.

My dad kept his promise that he would see me graduate, watching the live Internet broadcast of the ceremony from home. About one month later, he passed away. The grief was more intense than any pain I have ever felt, but it was tinged with relief. Dad's suffering was over, as was my family's constant stress over his health and my terrified anticipation of his death. During the five years since we lost my dad, my family and I have slowly worked our way back to each other from our separate corners of grief. I still have difficult days, when all I want is to have my dad back, but now those are far outnumbered by the days when I have a memory of Dad that makes me smile, or even laugh. I have been relieved to find that a world without Dad is not a world entirely without joy.

Questions for Reflection

Please reflect on and/or write out answers to the following questions:

1. When you consider your grief experience(s), which life transitions (e.g., graduation, marriage) most readily come to mind? How has your grief been expressed during your life transitions so far? What other future transitions do you believe will understandably highlight your grief?

2. How, if at all, do you believe your life transitions and/or your grief journey have been affected by the timing of your loss (before vs. during college), the cause of death (sudden vs. chronic) and/or the type of relationship with the person who died (family vs. friend)?

3. One of our authors shared that "Grief can feel huge and overwhelming, as if there is nothing that you can do to cope with it." She wanted to encourage you to think about how you cope with your grief during life transitions. What behaviors or thought processes do you turn to first? Which coping behavior or thought process do you find most helpful? How can you let others know how they can support you during these times?

For supporters:

What can you do to communicate and offer your support to grieving college students and young adults during particularly critical life transitions?

CHAPTER 7

Existential Questions about Self and Future

Experiencing the death of a loved one at any age often leaves grievers asking questions about their identity (i.e., Who am I now?), the future (i.e., What will life hold?), and how life works (i.e., purpose in life, religion or spirituality), now that their loved one is no longer physically present in their lives (Neimeyer, 2001).

Our authors described not wanting to be seen as a "griever," yet also wanting their death loss to be recognized as a life experience that significantly influenced who they were as a person. They communicated the need to not be defined by their grief, but also the idea that others could not truly know them without understanding the importance of their grief and the importance of their loved one who had died. With regard to the future, authors identified practical questions regarding shifts in roles and responsibilities within their family systems as well as concerns about their own future without the often unconditional love and support offered by their deceased loved one. In terms of sense-making about life, many indicated that questions about the meaning and purpose of life and about religion and spirituality were deeply intertwined with their grief. For many grievers, the death of a loved one can be connected with questions about how God could allow such a thing to occur. In contrast, many of our authors described comfort and consolation in their faith.

We have included the following three stories that we believe highlight the existential questions that often come up for grieving college students and young adults.

Charlene

Sex: Female

Age: 28

Time since death loss:
5 years, 3 months

During college

Death loss: Father

Gliobastoma multiforme cancer

In July 2004 my father—a commodities broker, world traveler, devoted Trekkie, and former assistant coach of my girls' junior softball team—started having dizzy spells. He went to the emergency room after one particularly bad spell and the physician told him it was an inner ear issue. He sought a second opinion and that's when we learned that he had a brain tumor. Additional tests revealed that it was glioblastoma multiforme, an aggressive cancer that has a high mortality rate. One of the worst moments of my life was when my parents called to tell me the diagnosis. It was between my freshman and sophomore years at the University of California, Berkeley (U.C. Berkeley), and my family lived in Florida. I curled up in the corner of my apartment with a blanket and spent the rest of the night sobbing so hard that my body shook.

A week later, I withdrew from the summer class I was taking and moved back to Florida. I officially transferred to the University of Central Florida so that I could be closer to my family during my father's surgery, radiation, and chemotherapy at the Mayo Clinic in Jacksonville. I struggled to understand why this was happening to us, and especially to my dad, who was well known for his generosity and humor. I loved and appreciated him too much for this to happen to him. I kept waiting to wake up and feel relief that this was all just a very bad dream. I never woke up.

When I withdrew from U.C. Berkeley to move back home to Florida, I was angry. I was angry that my father, who I had always had a close relationship with and admired, was now dealing with something so awful and scary. I felt crushed by "would" questions: Would my dad see me graduate? Would he be at my wedding in the future? Would he meet his grandchildren and get to enjoy a well-deserved retirement? Would my mom and two younger brothers be able to handle all of this?

U.C. Berkeley was my dream school and I was crushed when I left. Moving meant losing the support network of all my friends in California, and I became sullen and withdrawn. I stopped smiling. I applied for multiple jobs—I wanted at least three—so that I would be so busy that I wouldn't have to think about what was happening.

One of the hardest lessons I learned from my father's illness is that there are often ancillary losses. For example, my high school best friend and I were very close but my dad's illness changed our relationship. The optimistic, happy-go-lucky parts of me that laughed and loved life were gone. Ultimately we had a falling out and losing her friendship left me feeling even more broken.

Toward the end of my father's life, my mother fell apart. This is understandable given that she was about to lose her husband, best friend, and the father of her children. Unfortunately, she took this out on me and my brothers, and the pain of losing my dad was compounded by the fact that I was losing my mom too. When my dad was at home in hospice care a nurse left a box of prescriptions for us to give him when she wasn't there. We were supposed to administer them whenever we thought he needed them, like when he was in pain, but sometimes it wasn't clear if he needed them or not.

One night my mom woke me up by screaming at me and saying that my dad needed medicine. She yelled that I wasn't helping enough and that I should be watching him closer. "You need to help him! He's in pain and you're not doing anything! Can't you see what's going on?! Why aren't you doing anything?" She threw the medicine boxes at me. I never felt like a worse daughter. It was 3am and I thought that this must be what hell is like. My relationship with my mom changed after that moment, and it's still not the same. No one warned me that I would have to mourn the loss of my dad *and* the relationship with my mom.

One Friday I went to a hardware store and bought several cans of red paint, and I spent the weekend painting my bedroom walls the color that I felt inside all of the time. I cried a lot in the car, away from my family, so they wouldn't know how upset I was. I missed the person who I was before my dad got sick. I was sure that if someone opened me up there would be nothing inside; I was completely empty.

I was drawn to people who had lost a parent in their later teens or early twenties because I felt like they were the only ones who could understand how I felt. My supervisor at the time had lost her father and she comforted me in simple ways: calling to check up on me on days when I wasn't working, inviting me to go hiking so that I could vent my frustrations, and spending her lunch hour with me.

To this day I am still thankful for my grief counselor who helped me handle all of the emotions—from pain to bitterness—that I went through when my dad was sick and after he died. My appointments with her always gave me a sense of stability in the midst of chaos. I'd ring the doorbell, pour myself a cup of tea, sit on her couch, and express everything that I had held in for days. She never judged me and encouraged me to say whatever I wanted or needed to say. She helped me heal in ways that I never could have done by myself.

I'm action-oriented so what helped me during my grief journey was to help other people. I volunteered for brain tumor walks and a support network for grieving college students. I can't do anything to bring my father back, but I can help others who are going through a similar experience.

Kristen W.

Sex: Female

Age: 25

Time since death loss:
9 years, 3 months

Prior to college

Death loss: Mother

Breast cancer

When I was 12 years old, my mom was diagnosed with fourth stage breast cancer, the most advanced stage. After two years of harsh chemotherapy, physically grueling radiation, and a unilateral mastectomy, she was deemed "in remission." That day was the happiest day for my entire family, we breathed a sigh of relief and were able to focus on normal family things, like my brother's hockey games and my sister's recent graduation.

My family experienced relative normalcy for about four months, but unfortunately the cancer had come back with such a vengeance this time, as it moved from her breast and lymph nodes to her liver and brain.

It was October 23, 2003, a Thursday. I was headed home from another ordinary day as a sophomore in high school. A pit formed in my stomach as I turned on to our street and saw my sister's car parked in front of our house. My sister was not someone I had expected to see that day. I knew from the sight of her red GMC Jimmy that something big was happening inside the house. You see, my sister rarely made the trip home from college in the middle of the week, except for special occasions or extenuating circumstances. That day was one of those days for the unexpected.

Heading through the back door into the kitchen, I could see that something was not right in the family room. My dad, sister, aunt, and a close family friend were huddled around my mom who lay in the hospital bed that had been set up in the room a few weeks before. As I headed off to school that morning, something had been different as I kissed my mom's forehead and told her to have a good day; that morning she had not been responsive. The Do Not Resuscitate order hanging over her bed was an unholy reminder that we could lose her at any point in time.

At the age of 16, I had never imagined I would see my 45-year-old mom on her deathbed. The cancer had deteriorated her health and her poor body down to this weak and jaundiced condition. She had put up another two-year battle, but unfortunately was not going to be the victor this time. After her passing in the early hours of October 24, a lifelong journey of grief management began for everyone in my family.

My grief was primarily kept inside and rarely shared with others. In high school there were not many comfortable opportunities to share such personal experiences with the other students, so initially I managed things myself by processing the thoughts and emotions independently. My father had offered professional counseling for me and my siblings but allowed us to make the decision whether we wanted to use such services. I think this was incredibly beneficial to me as I was able to actively dictate how I would process my loss and grief. Even at the age of 16, I recognized that individuals process and express grief in very different ways, and really there is no "right" way.

Around the time of my mother's death, my fellow classmates were notified about the event by some of my teachers. This was helpful because I did not have to go back to school and explain to them why I had been absent for several days. There was one teacher, however, whose actions were not very supportive. He notified my fellow classmates but also encouraged them to give me my space and not talk to me because he believed I would become emotional. The rest of the school year was fairly uncomfortable and lonely in that class and I did not figure it out until the summer after my sophomore year when a new friend notified me about what the teacher had said. It is clear that he was well intentioned, but was somewhat misguided with his advice to my classmates.

The individuals who understood best what I was going through were those that could empathize. I had a very good friend in high school whose mother passed away about five months before my mother did. She and I could actually understand what the other was going through, not by offering sympathies but by bonding over the shared experience. As 16-year-old girls, we had to face the reality that our mothers would not be physically present at future events such as our junior prom, weddings, or when we had our own children one day. That is not a reality that most teenagers face, but having a friend who was going through the same event was incredibly meaningful and helped me through the initial shock of my mother's death.

Other friends who did not share this common thread were also extremely helpful with the coping process. I believe that having the balance of friends with and without shared experiences was vital to managing my grief. Sometimes I needed to talk about what I was thinking and feeling, that is when I valued my bond with my friend whose mom had also died. Most often I needed a distraction and an opportunity to get back to normalcy, which is where my general group of friends helped the most. They knew my story and what I was dealing with but did not focus on that or believe that that event defined me entirely as an individual. These friends allowed me to recognize that life goes on and that it is OK to laugh and be happy again.

Even in college I found incredibly supportive friends who understood what I had been through and always tried to recognize my mom and to bring her up at appropriate times even though they had never met her before. Those friends quickly learned which days were my saddest, and offered to help me through them by visiting the cemetery with me. One friend in particular always offers to go "visit my mom" when I need some clarity or reflection time.

Although I am and have been incredibly blessed to possess amazing support systems from both high school and college, there were some friendships that were not as strong or supportive. I had a very close friend whose mother was best friends with my mother. After my mom passed away that friend distanced herself and ignored me altogether. I lost my best friend on top of losing my mother. Our relationship has never recovered and she has not been in my life since I was 17. Reflecting back now, I think that she was not able to process her own grief and could no longer view me simply as me, she viewed me instead as the pitiable girl whose mother had died; someone she felt she could not share a connection with.

During my college career, I was able to become involved with campus-based organizations that were helpful to my journey through grief. First, I was able to participate in a small faith-sharing group in my dormitory, it was called *Cura Personalis*. This group was composed primarily of close friends from my hall and a wonderful peer minister and friend. I believe that *Cura* is responsible for the bonds that I still share with these individuals, they were able to get my back-story, and saw the true me from the very beginning of college.

I was also able to go on self-discovery focused Jesuit retreats. One in particular was called Kairos, I attended the retreat two times as a retreatant; this weekend retreat allowed me to hear stories from others and to reflect on my own. During my senior year, I was blessed with a position on the leadership team for Kairos, an opportunity that allowed me to offer my story to those attending the retreat. Kairos has been very therapeutic for me, both as a leader and a retreatant. It was also where I met the friend who would later help me to organize a support network for grieving students at our university.

As reflected in the groups I elected to be involved in, I believe faith and religion were invaluable in supporting me along my grief journey. One of my favorite inspirational quotes is from Bernadette Devlin McAliskey: "The will of God will never take you where the grace of God will not protect you." Keeping this belief in sight has allowed my grief to be more manageable and helped me focus on the "bigger picture."

Shirin

Sex: Female

Age: 21

Time since death loss:
4 years, 2 months

Prior to college

Death loss: Sister

Car accident

"Just when the caterpillar thought the world was over, it became a butterfly."

This is my favorite quote and I feel that it reflects my story, though it is still being written, as I have yet to become a full-blown butterfly. However, I have come a long way, and am growing and changing constantly. I have been to the lowest of the low, to a dark place where I no longer wanted to live, and I survived it.

There is much more to my story than just my "loss." It begins when my family and I moved to America when I was six years old, leaving the rest of our family behind. I couldn't speak English and express my thoughts, I looked different, and I was picked on. This, along with my own personal characteristics, had an impact on the coping mechanisms I adopted, such as internalizing. I have struggled with self-esteem, body image issues, and depression. All of the changes and struggles, along with my relationships, influenced my grief story.

A little over a week before I started my senior year in high school, I lost my big sister, Sheila, in a car accident. I had been hanging out with my friends that day. When I got home, I saw my sister briefly; she was about to leave to go to her boyfriend's house. She wanted the keys for my dad's small car, which were in my room, so I told her to take her truck. She reluctantly agreed and then she left with just a "see you later."

About two hours later, we got a phone call from the hospital letting us know that my sister was in ICU. My mom panicked, my dad screamed, and I tried to hold it together, assuring them that everything was fine. I was angry that my sister did something stupid to end up in the hospital to worry the whole family, but I also couldn't help but think *if only she had taken my dad's car instead of her truck.* I was in shock because I never thought anything like this would happen. On the way to the hospital, we passed her truck on the opposite side of the street. It was upright and not even dented, so I "knew" everything was OK. When I entered the hospital, the waiting room had a strange feel to it. My parents were on opposite ends of the room and a few minutes passed before the doctor came to tell us Sheila didn't make it. It hit me like a ton of bricks and at that moment, the world I knew fell apart. I cannot describe the feelings and thoughts I had, but life from that moment on became surreal. My mom was crying and my dad was screaming on the floor begging for my sister to come back. I did not know how to comfort my parents as I hadn't really done so before, since we weren't ever close.

We soon learned that while we were sitting at home, about two miles down the road were ambulances, helicopters, and firetrucks because of the major accident. My sister had died on impact after swerving into oncoming traffic.

Soon, we were notifying friends, who came to the hospital. Many were hysterical, but not as much as my dad. It became momentarily real when I saw her body, and I never wanted to leave her, but we had to eventually.

The days following the accident were the hardest, most unreal days of my life. I couldn't take it. About a week later, I went on with life and put aside my grief. School had started and I did not want to be the "girl who lost her sister." Before, I mostly kept to myself and was not involved with many after-school organizations. However, everyone knew my sister, so I ended up being "the girl who lost her sister" anyway. I became very self-conscious in school, and felt like everyone was watching me, so I couldn't be myself. I put on a face, and that face has been hard to strip. I had become disconnected from my emotions, so my life events were just "facts" that I could speak about.

Many times I felt guilty for not grieving and "not missing" my sister. I justified my feelings, or lack of them, with the fact that my sister and I weren't very close; I do not remember ever saying "I love you" to her. When we fought, it was violent and got so bad to the point where we told each other "I wish you died!" But, the truth is, my sister was the only person who ever truly knew me, the only one who came close to knowing my inner/family struggles. She was there through everything with me. I could be myself with her; she loved me very much and was my number one fan. To add to the pain and shame, I couldn't help feeling that the wrong sister died. So many people loved my sister. She knew how to brighten someone's day, make anyone laugh, and she had big plans for her future. This all made dealing with the loss more difficult, and contributed to me pushing aside my grief, convincing myself that the loss was not affecting me.

My tendency to try to "do life on my own" had a greater impact than ever before. Before the accident, I kept everything inside and I acted out my emotions in solitude and in destructive ways like violence. After the accident, I couldn't deal with these powerful emotions the same ways as I had done before, so I disconnected from myself, my emotions, and my life. The bigger problem was that no one on the outside knew.

I soon learned that numbness has its own pain. That year, I started taking drugs so I could bring my emotions to the forefront and "deal with them." I was tired of living but not feeling alive. I felt like getting high was OK because I was self-medicating. I could grieve, and I could see the bigger picture; life made sense.

When I started at the University of Georgia, I entered into the hardest year of my life. Going somewhere where most people didn't know me, my loss became like a secret; I rarely brought it up. Often, people asked if I had any siblings and I either told them "I don't," or I would say "I did but she died"; the latter created an uncomfortable situation. I just didn't know what to do with these cards I was dealt. My destructive habits continued through college, where I partied often and got involved with a crowd and lifestyle that brought me further away from myself. I got in a lot of trouble, and I finally had enough in my junior year. I began putting more focus into organizations and volunteer work that would aid in my healing. The most significant on-campus groups for me included AMF, a support network for grieving students, African American Choral Ensemble, and Christian Campus Fellowship (CCF).

I became active member of CCF, a campus ministry where I found a home away from home. Through this organization, my eyes were opened to how God is there through life's struggles and how much community can help with healing. I am able to express some emotions when I worship, and have found other constructive ways to cope. For me, these other ways include helping others and partaking in hobbies I enjoy, such as being in nature, running, exercising, and dancing. Writing had helped me from the start, as I wrote to my sister after the accident. I still love to write, whether it is poetry, free writing, or song writing. Music has also been a huge part of my life and my healing. I love to sing, and I know that my sister wants me to continue singing.

I feel that the phrase "lost and found" is optimal in describing what happened to me, since losing my sister sparked my journey to find myself. I am now substance free and have found ways to feel "high" without drugs. I have transformed into a completely new person. There is still the part of me that feels I can do it alone and that wants to be "independent." But, I know that to heal and truly be strong, I need to face my pain, talk about my feelings and be vulnerable with others. I am learning how to have deeper relationships and open up to people without drugs. This involves me having more compassion for myself.

The ironic thing is that, through Sheila's death, I have learned what it means to live. I try to enjoy each day and live fully like she did. This doesn't mean I don't struggle with old insecurities sometimes or that I deal with everything the right way and always make the right decisions. But now, I am not my own enemy. It means I am beginning to spread my wings and try to be the best person I can be.

My relationships with my parents, as well as my relationship with myself, have also improved drastically. I have even realized that my relationship with my sister has not ended, but has transformed as well. I see Sheila often in my dreams, and we communicate in other ways as well, such as through music or through others. She will always have a place in my heart that can never ever be filled. I will forever feel that a part of me is missing. But now, I can look back at a dream, and instead of crying about how I miss her, I can laugh about the message. It's not easy accepting that this has to be our relationship, but it is better than nothing. When I think it's too much to take, I can take a deep breath in. Then exhale. In the end, what I have been through has shaped the butterfly I am becoming.

Questions for Reflection

Please reflect on and/or write out answers to the following questions:

1. What questions, if any, have you asked about who you are as a person since your loved one died?

2. What existential (i.e., bigger than ourselves) questions (e.g., why do bad things happen to good people?), if any, have you asked since your loved one died?

3. Who do you turn to for assistance with these types of deep questions? What type of support has helped you the most when you have thought about these kinds of questions? What type has helped you the least?

For supporters:

What are some ways that you can support and assist grieving college students and young adults who are dealing with existential questions?

CHAPTER 8

Importance of Connecting
with a Mentor

Although there is not much attention within the grief literature on mentors or mentorship, mentors' potential for having positive impact on youth and young adults is well documented (DuBois *et al.*, 2011). Many of the authors emphasized and expressed gratitude for the assistance of a mentor in their lives.

These mentors were often adults from their extended family (e.g., aunt, uncle) or an unrelated adult (e.g., coach, family friend) who were most helpful through their consistent presence, availability, and nonjudgmental attitude. Many of the mentors were also grieving the same loss (e.g., uncle grieving his brother's death) or had experienced a significant loss in their own lives. In these cases, the mentor served as a wise peer. In other cases, the mentors were adults (e.g., co-workers, professors) who simply had more life experience and seemed to be in a place where they could offer an empathic ear when others (e.g., family members, non-grieving peers) were just not able to do so. For college students, having a professor to turn to who could also advocate on their behalf was extremely valuable. For young adults following college, we believe that similar mentors perhaps within their workplace could also be quite valuable.

Though not included in the stories in this section, a few authors shared their experience of the truly negative blow that can occur when someone they considered to be a mentor, particularly if also a professor, was insensitive or unsupportive during their grief.

We have included the following two stories that we believe highlight the importance of mentors in lives of grieving college students and young adults.

Katherine

Sex: Female

Age: 26

Time since death loss:
11 years, 6 months

Prior to college

Death loss: Father

Liver failure

A few months into my freshman year of high school, I was told my father (who everyone called Timmy) was sick. The way I remember it, my mom and other family members did not want my brother and me to have much information in order "to protect us." To this day I am not sure when they actually knew he was terminally ill. He was in and out of the hospital several times but the adults decided it would be too hard for us to see him. When we finally were allowed to see him, he was bright yellow with jaundice due to cirrhosis and liver failure; still, no one told my brother and me what the long-term prognosis was. Being young and naïve, I assumed the doctors would fix whatever was wrong with him and he would go back to being my same old dad. Then he was transferred to another hospital several hours away, and after balancing work and school schedules, we only made it there a few times. He was getting weaker and frailer, but I still thought he was going to be fine.

Then at the end of May, my mom told us we were going to the hospital the next day. I knew this did not bode well because it would mean missing school which she never allowed. My dad did not want to be on life support or go to any extreme measures, but my uncle knew my dad would want the family to be there to say goodbye so they had him intubated and on dialysis for several days until we all could get there.

The whole family arrived at the hospital and we were brought into the family room where the doctors told us the only remaining option was a liver transplant, but that my dad was likely too ill to receive one. I was blind-sided. Part of me probably knew that this was possible, but I felt like I had no warning that this was the end. We all took turns saying goodbye as they turned off the ventilator and watched as he slowly slipped away. I'll never forget when it was my turn and I started whispering in his ear, my uncle said, "Katy, he knows it's you, his heart rate just jumped up!" The nurse finally said, "His heart is still beating a little but he's pretty much gone." I kept holding his hand until they made us leave because I didn't want to let it get cold. I felt confused, angry, guilty, and empty all at the same time. I had no idea what to do.

I stayed home from school the next day, while my guidance counselor told my class that my father had died. When I returned, people were nice enough and expressed sympathy but no one really wanted to get too close, just in case death was contagious. I became very withdrawn from my friends and couldn't seem to enjoy anything. I didn't talk about his death with even my closest friends because we were all too scared and had no idea what to say. So I locked my feelings up. My parents were divorced so none of my friends really knew my dad. That made it easier, on the outside, to act like my dad never existed. But on the inside, my grief consumed me.

For years, my grief was mainly expressed internally. I did not want to show my pain, so I would hide it. I became very withdrawn and quiet when I had been fairly outgoing before my dad's death. It was like I didn't want to talk about anything in case my feelings all started spilling out. I was so depressed and exhausted all the time, and I didn't want to waste my energy talking to people. I started eating lunch alone at my high school; my house was essentially silent because my mom, brother, and I essentially stopped talking to each other. Everyone's denial made me feel abandoned and crazy, like there was something wrong with me for being sad.

My dad's brother was the most understanding person after my dad's death. He had lost his big brother, and like the rest of the family seemed to have very little idea how to cope. I spent most of my free time at his house around the corner from my own. He seemed to be the only person who was not afraid to admit being sad, missing my dad, and feeling in despair. He would say my dad's name out loud, which everyone else seemed afraid to do, and this gave me profound comfort. It made me feel like I was not crazy, that he did actually die and we were actually dealing with this.

My main outlet in high school was staying active. I had always been a good student, and I continued to get all As through high school. I played soccer year round, and was on the varsity winter and spring track team. As soon as I got my driver's license, I got a job and would be out of the house from 6:30am until 10:30pm.

Three-and-a-half years after my dad died, I started college at Georgetown University. It did not take long for my buried emotions to rise to the surface. With all of the introductions, "get to know you" games, and parent events, I realized that although no one at home knew how to deal with his death and pretended everything was fine, at least they *knew* my dad had died. Now I was faced with explaining it to dozens of new people. I often would answer questions about my parents by just saying "my mom…" and letting people wonder. I didn't want to start out my friendships being "the girl whose dad died." It was extremely painful to hear people talk about their dads, and I was so jealous of them. I used my old approach of staying active and started playing rugby. This quickly became the expression of my many feelings. Rugby was also my dad's passion for over thirty years, so when I play rugby I feel more connected to him than any other time.

I considered going to the university counseling center, but really just wanted to talk to people like me, not a therapist. It was probably one of the best days of my life when I read in an email about a student starting a peer-led grief support group. I attended the first meeting and felt a little awkward. But very quickly it became clear that I was with people who understood my feelings, who had been there, and who also wanted to connect with other students going through the same thing. We started bi-monthly support group meetings and I would literally count the days until the next one. I would get through the pain and emptiness by knowing I had a meeting soon. At the meetings, I felt like I could finally relax fully, take a deep breath, and feel comfortable. I could just feel it when I walked in the room that everyone got it. I was not a freak, I was not alone, I was not crazy for still being so affected four years later.

Since I had never actually talked about my grief, it was terrifying at first. There were a number of meetings when I didn't say anything at all. I knew I would immediately start crying and was scared of being that vulnerable. I also struggled with the notion that since my father was an alcoholic, people would think it was his fault he died. I didn't think I had a right to be as upset as people whose parents had cancer, ALS, or heart attacks. But even when I didn't talk, it was so therapeutic to hear other people say the exact thoughts racing through my mind. Although every person's journey of grief is different, there are also so many similarities that are very unifying.

During my junior year of college, I experienced another blow when my best friend's father died of a heart attack in his sleep, very suddenly and unexpectedly. My close friends and I were completely shell-shocked. For days, we all slept together on the couch and cried with my friend when she woke up in the middle of the night sobbing. This death amplified my grief more than I thought possible; when my friend's dad died all the emotions that I buried and refused to let out just exploded. I went back to Georgetown a week late because of the funeral and was severely depressed all semester. I spent a lot of time in bed, failed several exams, and didn't really care. The support group was my savior during this time. I felt somewhat selfish for being so upset when it was not my own family member, but everyone was so incredibly supportive and understanding. It was like I was finally grieving the loss of my dad, and in a healthier way.

In addition, my rugby coach in college became my mentor, closest confidante, and best friend. I don't remember how I even told her about my dad, but it always came up at rugby because rugby was my dad's passion and the reason I started playing. As soon as she knew this, she asked all about him, which no one else ever did. Many people assume it is too painful to talk about and don't want to make you upset. But I yearned for people to ask about him. She also asked when he died and when his birthday was and continues to check in with me on those days. I don't think any of my best friends even know these dates, and this means a tremendous amount to me. She still acknowledges how hard it is and understands how big of a deal it was and is for me to talk about him. Recently, I posted a picture of my dad and me on Facebook for the first time, and she told me how proud she was of me. To most people, this was a totally normal event but for me posting this picture was a big deal. She understands grief is a journey, and supports me in whatever phase I happen to be in on any given day.

One of the most unexpected reactions throughout my grief was anger. I was so angry with my friends for not being there for me when my dad died. Yes we were young, but why could no one figure out that all they had to do was hug me, or sit with me and watch TV, or honestly ask how I was feeling? Soon, I was crushed when I found out that another of my friends' fathers had died. My friends and I were inseparable for a week after the funeral. Once we were all back at school, I would call them and check in. We visited their graves together on break. And eventually we had several conversations about how horrible they felt for not being there for me years prior. It was comforting to know they regretted their absence, but also amplified my feeling of "why me." Once again, the group was incredibly comforting. Hearing other members' experience with some of the same anger and confusion regarding friends made me feel normal for once.

When I graduated, I was extremely sad to be without the support group. I almost felt spoiled for having had such an amazing support system all four years of college. I feared I would once again be alone in my grief. I was lucky to find a friend whose father died almost the same month mine did, and we became very close. But even now, over 11 years later, I struggle to talk about my dad. When I know I want to say something about him, I get flushed and short of breath and my heart races. It seems too painful to say things out loud but I have forced myself because otherwise I am afraid I will forget them. I don't want to forget the memories we made, or forget the things he said and did. I don't want him to think I am ashamed of him. I want to feel natural telling a story about my dad when other people are telling stories about theirs. Someday, I want to be able to tell my kids about him without crying. I *still* just want to feel normal again.

Many people think that grieving is done in a certain period of time, that after a few weeks or months they can stop asking how you are feeling and assume you are fine. But I love when people ask about my dad because, though it is still painful to talk about him, it is very comforting to have someone acknowledge the loss and care.

Brent

Sex: Male

Age: 27

Time since death loss: 15 years

Prior to college

Death loss: Father

Heart attack

For me, since my loss occurred when I was younger (at age 12), my story of grief as a college student is more about a situation where I was finally tending to feelings and emotions that I buried after the "incident." That being—I lost my father in middle school as the result of a heart attack. Although I think a lot of the grieving process was dealt with then, I often tried to be "tough" in dealing with my personal tragedy. I tried hard not to show emotion, not to talk about it much, and to just sort of be strong in continuing my everyday life. If there is anything I can pass along to someone else dealing with a similar sort of tragedy, it's to talk about it. Talk about it with your family, your friends, a counselor, anyone. It is healthy. Not weak. It takes a bigger person to face their feelings rather than suppress them.

Personally, I think I took a lot of my grief out through sports. I played harder, maybe even meaner, and definitely more emotional in both football and basketball. Although this may sound like a positive, it wasn't always, as it left me at odds with coaches at times. On the other hand, in retrospect, I noticed that my mindset and work ethic in school dropped tremendously. Before my father's death, I was a straight A student and took it all very seriously. However, after his death, it was tough to take on schoolwork with the same sense of importance.

Sometimes dealing with teachers was difficult. They had their agendas and their lesson plans and, to be honest, I just lost my father and I couldn't care less about some insignificant homework assignment. Sometimes that was challenging to deal with.

In contrast, my middle school football coach was really supportive. He had three of us on his team (me, my twin, and my older brother) and he sort of just kept an eye out for us. Small things but they meant a lot. One of the coolest examples of this was when my brother printed out stickers with my father's initials (J.R.C.) on them, and our coach had all the players put them on their helmets for the next game. I've always cherished that.

Sometimes I think I envied friends of mine who still had both parents and who didn't realize how good they had it. Although these thoughts were generally fleeting, I think it's important to not be too shameful of these, or any kind of similar thoughts. The grieving process can be a complicated one and I would simply suggest you try not to hold your natural negative feelings from such a tragedy against those who care about you. Instead, try to process them in a healthy way as best you can.

Luckily, I'm part of a large family. So I had four other kids that "got it" to a degree as well. I think having brothers and sisters all dealing with the same event was a huge help in my grieving process. I was fortunate to have that. I could not imagine taking on something like this alone. And if you are alone, I think it's so important to find people who do "get it," that you can talk to. Easier said than done, I know, but it is possible. We all need people to provide an outlet to help heal our wounds.

Being part of a peer-lead support group during college was honestly one of the most comfortable ways I've ever gotten to deal with my grief. To connect with people my age that could understand what I was going through was an enormous aid in gaining closure on my father's death. And yes, as clichéd as that may sound, it's the truth. It wasn't a pity party where everyone whined and cried. It was real. People talking out issues, how they coped, suggestions to help others, and how to take the positive away from whatever tragedy you may have gone through.

Questions for Reflection

Please reflect on and/or write out answers to the following questions:

1. Who, if anyone, served or is serving as a mentor in your grief? Be as open as possible in your definition of a mentor. It could be someone who is a role model and/or someone who may not even know that he or she is a mentor to you. How has this person helped?

2. How might you connect with other mentors and/or serve as a mentor yourself?

For supporters:

What are some ways that you mentor the grieving college students and young adults in your life? How can you help them connect with other mentors?

CHAPTER 9

Life Lessons Learned

Some of the most profound lessons about life can be learned through experiencing death losses. Most of the authors shared at least one life lesson they learned from their loss and/or from the way their loved one lived his or her life—lessons they could take with them as they moved forward in their grief and their lives.

Examples of these lessons included heightened valuing of interpersonal relationships, increased confidence in their ability to cope with life stressors, reorganization of life priorities, and enhanced clarity regarding their purpose in life. There was a sense of transformation in many of the stories, a movement from grief as devastation to grief as, although something they never would have chosen, an experience with some value. A few authors seemed to want to derive meaning out of their difficult experience. These life lessons were at times related to the authors' sense of enhanced maturity (see Chapter 3) and, therefore, sometimes contributed to their sense of separateness from their peers. A few other authors (not in this chapter) demonstrated that they learned major life lessons through the decisions that they made, but they did not specifically state that they had learned life lessons.

We have included the following three stories that we believe highlight the life lessons often experienced by grieving college students and young adults.

Danielle C.

Sex: Female

Age: 23

Time since death loss:
3 years, 7 months

During college

Death loss: Father

Brain cancer

I lost my dad to brain cancer on April 7, 2009. At 6am, I woke to a call from my mom saying my dad didn't make it. I remember tears flooding my eyes as I tried to answer my mom with a steady voice. I was on my bed, my knee to my chest and my roommate and best friend's arms around me. The three months preceding that phone call were a whirlwind of doctors' appointments, talks with specialists, and...struggle.

New Year's Day my dad was rushed to the emergency room for what we thought was a stroke. My dad was never one to make a fuss over himself, so when my mom asked him if she should call an ambulance and he nodded a reply, I knew something was wrong. I sat with him, our dog in his lap and a blank stare in his eyes. I remember one of the older paramedics telling me that now was the time I needed to be strong. To this day I think about him and his message to me. Like he knew what I was about to face and was sent to prepare me. My dad lost a lot of his functioning, ability to communicate, and cognitive skills throughout all the surgeries and radiation treatments. There was never a point when he was truly stable or back to his "normal." That January morning was the last time I saw my dad the way I had always known him to be. Despite all of this, he kept assuring us that he was fine and things were going to be OK. Through everything, he was always the one telling us, "Everything's gonna be OK."

I couldn't grasp what was happening. The man I saw in the hospital bed looked like my dad, sounded like my dad, but there was a wall. He was somewhere deep inside, but there was something missing when we talked to him. His journey was filled with complication after complication and more hills and valleys than I ever thought possible. A surgery would be successful and then he would throw a clot. He'd be discharged home, but then begin having seizures. The highs were filled with hope and the lows were crushing. But through everything, the people in my dad's life who loved him—and there were a lot of them!—were there. Family, friends, and friends who might as well be family stepped up in ways unthinkable. I love each and every one of them for the role they played in his battle.

One of the most difficult things to deal with was being in college and coping with what was going on at home. My dad wanted me to stay in school, so I made the four-hour round trip commute each weekend; sometimes I came in the middle of the week after receiving phone calls telling me I should come home and say goodbye, because this time might be it. I didn't take a single exam that semester on the date that it was scheduled and for about three months I slept three to four hours per night. Every night, when I turned off the lights and closed my eyes, my mind was flooded with grief, fear, and sadness. As soon as my head hit the pillow, tears filled my eyes. I would force myself out of bed to run away from the pain. Looking back now, it's almost comical the lengths I would go for a little shut-eye. I needed background noise to mute my even noisier mind, so I slept in the common room with the TV on. Then I found myself becoming interested in what was on, so the Food Network was tuned to a gentle volume level four. Then the light from the flames on the stoves would be too much stimulus, so I grabbed a bandana and tied it over my eyes. I wish I could have seen my roommates' reactions the first morning they found me on the couch, blindfolded, with Emeril Lagasse practically on mute. Regardless of how ridiculous it looked, it worked! I was slowly able to wean myself back into a normal sleep pattern, although it took time. But, like so many other things I found surrounding the loss of a loved one, grief does not work on our timeline, it follows one of its own.

I struggled to hold myself together during the time that my dad was sick and the years after he passed away. I worked every day to be strong for my family, to keep a smile on my face for my friends, and to give my all to my classes and extracurricular commitments. But the person who held me together at the seams every time I felt that I would surely come undone was my then boyfriend and now husband. He was the one who saw me most broken, who held me as I cried myself to sleep, who allowed me to fall apart in his arms after

I was exhausted from holding myself together. I was blessed that he had the chance to know my dad for four years before he passed away, and that my dad had the chance to meet the man I married.

That semester my dad was sick, my roommates were flawless. They worked behind the scenes, like a synchronized team, making my day-to-day life just a little more manageable. My phone would ring and they would jump into action. One had a bag ready with all my essential belongings, another had packed me food and made me tea, and the third had her keys in hand ready to drive me home. Those girls were my angels those four months and I could never thank them enough for what they did. I couldn't have managed without them in my life then, and still couldn't today.

In terms of my family, my brother is so strong, so resilient, and underneath his armor lies such a warm heart. The relationship I gained with my brother was one of the greatest blessings my dad could have given us. Looking back now, I know it was one of his many parting gifts for us. My brother is truly the man of our household now and has earned that position. I know that my dad would be so proud of the man he has become. He truly is his father's son. My mom is beautiful, inside and out. She is a strong and fearless leader in every aspect of her life. She seamlessly took on the role of caregiver for my dad and was so incredible in that role, never giving up hope, always loving, and always pushing forward.

For a young person, I had come to know far too many grown-up experiences and began to feel very alone and isolated in my grief. I was on a campus surrounded by 20,000 other students; students I was sure couldn't begin to grasp what I was dealing with. It wasn't until my dad passed away and I began talking to the people around that I started to realize that this might not be the case. I found that so many other students had experiences like mine. They came to me and comforted me, told me it was going to be hard, but I'd get through, and that they sometimes still struggled. These students, my peers and my friends, they too had had these very adult experiences much sooner than anyone should have to. They too knew what loss meant.

I benefited so much from getting to know grieving peers through a support network for grieving students. I also was involved in amazing service projects while my dad was sick and after he died. It was about a month after I found out that my dad was sick that I signed up a team for our university's chapter of Relay for Life. Relay for Life is a volunteer-led event dedicated to raising money for cancer research and celebrating cancer survivors across the United States. Something inside me hesitated to make that reservation for a team—about three weeks before the event, my dad lost his battle with cancer. I was ready to pull out of the entire thing, let someone else run the team, but yet again found that the moment I reached out, I was absolutely overwhelmed by the response (e.g., bypassing the donation goal, my family traveling to be there, my roommates making t-shirts).

My dad was a true Renaissance man, full of passion and life. He played bass in a garage band with his best friends from childhood and my uncles, he loved photography, he coached and went to every sporting event my brother and I had, and gave standing ovations at all of my plays. He was a dancer, a cook, a sailor, street smart from growing up in Philly and book smart earning his Master's degree. He was the best man you could have been lucky enough to know and my biggest fan. I know he still watches over me. When I look out at the ocean and begin to feel tears in my eyes, missing my dad, and a wave comes and soaks my jeans to my knees, I know that's his way of telling me to "cut it out and smile." I hope I never get over the loss of my dad. I hope I grow. I hope I continue to remember his legacy, what he taught me, his words, his laugh, and his voice. I hope I make him proud. I am a better person because I am his daughter. He taught me to be strong. He taught me to be passionate. Most of all, he taught me to find joy in pain and allowed me to come out on the other side of tragedy, knowing "everything's gonna be OK."

Kaitlyn

Sex: Female

Age: 22

Time since death loss:
10 years, 8 months

Prior to college

Death loss: Father

Heart attack

Before I entered first grade, my parents divorced. I was young and didn't really understand the new life I was thrown into. My mom and I moved out, and I was only able to see my dad every other weekend. I had been used to not seeing my dad very often, as he had been in the Navy. He eventually left the service to watch me grow up.

As my dad and I were only able to spend time together on the weekends, we would make the most out of it—we went to amusement parks, played mini golf, and we'd make midnight runs for snacks. My dad was my best friend and I was Daddy's Girl. We'd parade around town in matching sweatshirts, and go to the local diner on Sundays for breakfast. My dad even made the other kids at school jealous by sending gorgeous flowers to my classroom every Valentine's Day. My dad's love for me is the most powerful love I've ever witnessed. Only, I had no idea that this would all end before I even turned 12 years old.

Most of my time was spent living with my mom. On May 30, 2002, my mom had to do something no parent should ever have to. Just past 3am, she opened my bedroom door and woke me up. Tears filled her eyes as she told me, "Dad had a heart attack." At that moment, I became wide awake and asked, "What hospital is he at?" Mom took a moment to answer before saying, "He's in Heaven." I later learned he died of a fatal arrhythmia. I was absolutely devastated. He was only 37 years old, and he was home alone when it happened. Though he did always say, "Life is short," it never even crossed my mind that I would lose him.

It's been over 10 years since that day. Losing my dad was the most devastating experience I've ever had to deal with. It was so completely unexpected and sudden. But I know for a fact I would not be the person I am today if he had never been a part of my life. He taught me many valuable lessons, and even though I only knew him for 11 years I am so thankful that he was my dad.

Our relationships with others define who we are. For me, the most influential person in my life has been my father for many reasons. Even though I wasn't able to see him that much, my dad kept teaching me right from wrong, and for that I am thankful. I believe I am a strong person because of the lessons my dad taught me. He taught me a lot about life and values. One of the most important lessons he taught me was to never quit. He believed quitting showed weakness and that wasn't a quality he wanted me to possess. He also always told me education was very important, and I believe his words helped me earn my Bachelor's degree two years ago from the University of Rhode Island, *cum laude.*

As a child and teenager, I was lucky enough to have a nonprofit organization called FRIENDS Way (Families Reaching into Each New Day) to help me through my grieving process. FRIENDS Way is a bereavement center for children and families dealing with the death of a loved one. I don't know where I'd be without them. I found it difficult to talk about my loss with my friends at school because they just didn't understand. The support group meetings allowed me to realize that there are other people out there who feel the same way I did, and they also gave me a safe place to share these feelings.

It was at a FRIENDS Way meeting that I first learned about National Students of AMF, a support network for grieving students. They were starting a chapter at my college, and I knew it was something that I had to be a part of. I attended almost every meeting, although the group had just begun and not many students knew about it. Most of the time it would just be the co-presidents and me. The following year I became the president of the chapter, but unfortunately I was unable to get the word out on my own. It was heartbreaking not being able to establish a successful chapter, but I am so thankful for David and all of the other wonderful people I had the opportunity to meet at two of the AMF conferences.

My dad's passing has been connected with my college experience in other ways too. I was taking my first film production course and it was time to propose to the class what we had chosen to make for our final project. I had known for a while what I wanted to do, which was a music video to a song, entitled "Father's Day" by my favorite band Stephen Kellogg and the Sixers. The song had always held a special place in my heart. For a while I would listen to this song and picture a story unfolding about my life and how I have dealt with the loss of my dad. I was afraid to tell the class that I was planning on making something so personal, as they were all doing narrative stories that they wrote. My professor, Keith, was not a fan of students doing music videos, but he was open to me doing it.

For the film, I planned on cutting together old home videos of my dad and me with footage I would shoot of my seven-year-old cousin Railey walking around the cemetery where my dad is buried. Railey would be representing a younger version of myself. She was born a few months after my dad passed away, so she's always been a visual representation of how long he's been gone. My plan was to project the old home videos on a screen and to then re-film them off the wall using black and white 16mm film in a Bolex camera, whereas the shots of Railey would be filmed in color Super 8 film.

The first day of filming went pretty smoothly. I really did not have a solid plan for what I wanted to film that day, and since I was using a Super 8 camera I had no way of looking at the footage until after it was processed at the lab. I had some very mixed emotions while filming that day. I felt anxious that I was filming at the place where my dad was buried, and soon my class would see one of the most personal aspects of my life, but I also felt an inexplicable sense of peace. This was also the first time that my fiancé Anthony (my boyfriend at the time) had visited the cemetery with me.

When I saw the footage for the first time after it came back from the lab, I was amazed. The shots were more beautiful than I had could have imagined. While editing, everything fell together seamlessly; somehow the shots fit together beautifully with the music. At the beginning of the film you can hear my dad saying something about me, so I decided to end the film with my voice saying, "I love you, Daddy."

On the night of the final film screening, I was unbearably nervous. Not only was I about to share such a personal story with my classmates, but also with a room full of strangers as we were encouraged to invite friends and family to the screening. My mom and Anthony sat on either side of me as my film began to play on the giant projection screen in the auditorium. My hands squeezed both of theirs as hard as I could. I could not breathe, and I am pretty sure that everyone in that room could hear my heart pounding. When the screen went black, I felt an overwhelming sense of relief. The applause and sniffling I heard from the audience made it all worth it.

Deciding to make such a personal film about my life was undoubtedly one of the biggest risks I have ever taken. By allowing myself to be vulnerable and expressing my grief in my own way, I have been able to touch many people. Because of this film, I was nominated and chosen by faculty to receive the first ever Fred Joyal Film/Media award for Excellence in Production. I also had the opportunity to show my film to Stephen Kellogg and the Sixers after one of their shows. It meant so much to me that they took the time to watch something so personal, and I was surprised that Stephen cried while watching it. The band loved it so much that they decided to release it as their official music video on their website.

I miss my dad every day and I know he's watching down on me. It's so heartbreaking that he was never able to accomplish everything he wanted to. He always told me that life was short and those are the words I try to live by. I will do everything in my power to make him proud, and that's all I can do to thank him.

Leah

Sex: Female

Age: 22

Time since death loss:
3 years, 10 months

Prior to college

Death loss: Father

Heart attack

My dad died at the end of July 2009 when I was 18 years old, and I started college in September that year. He died suddenly of a massive heart attack while he was out for a run. He was an avid runner and ran every day. It was unexpected and we found out later that he had an earlier heart attack that went undetected and undiagnosed; it probably didn't seem like anything more than the stomach flu.

My younger sister, who was 15, and I were in New Orleans for a retreat when my dad died and we flew back home the next morning with my pastor. The whole funeral process was a blur. In fact, I don't remember much of anything until Welcome Week at Northwestern University two months later. I did not tell my freshman advisor or the members of my orientation group what I was going through. I was more reserved and quieter than I was before and had trouble making friends. The only person I told about my dad was my roommate and that was simply because I wanted to explain why my uncle helped me move in instead of my dad and why I cried myself to sleep every night.

Many times, when I tried to talk to people about my dad it did not turn out well. I stopped talking about his death and treated it like a secret. For example, I became friends with a guy who lived down the hall freshman year. He seemed nice enough and we got along well. One night, after I started sobbing after watching the "wishing you were somehow here again" scene from *The Phantom of the Opera*, a song that expresses *exactly* the way it feels to lose a father, I explained to him how and when my dad died. His response was to take a copy of a religious text off his shelf and start evangelizing to me, telling me how his religion views death. I think he meant to comfort me, but it made me defensive; I was in a vulnerable position and felt like he was trying to convert me. The next year, I chose not to tell my new roommate until a few months after we moved in together. After I told her about my dad, she said, "Oh, I already knew" and then grilled me about how my family and I were handling it. She asked if I looked down on people who used antidepressants to alleviate the grieving process. I was horrified at her complete lack of understanding of the complexity of grief, and our relationship was strained for the rest of the year.

The complexity of my grief has come out through a range of feelings, thoughts, and actions. I get bitter and angry when people talk negatively about their parents and take their family for granted, because all I can think about is the fact that they still have both their parents. During events like family weekends and Father's Day activities, I struggle with feelings of loneliness. Socially, I want to go out with friends and party less often. When I first arrived on campus, I made a conscious decision not to drink. I knew that if I wasn't careful, I could end up relying on alcohol to numb my feelings, and I knew just how dangerous that could be. I also felt guilty because I felt that it was wrong to go out and party when I was supposed to be grieving. I found it difficult to be too happy because it felt like I was forgetting about my dad.

There were times I would throw myself into my studies as a way to avoid dealing with my emotions. I always enjoyed school and never had a problem doing my homework, but there have been many nights over the last four years when I would tell myself that I couldn't think about my dad or spend time dealing with how I feel because I needed to focus on school. I think some of it was overcompensation. I put a lot of effort in at times so that I could let myself skip class later if I was having a bad day. I also never wanted to be seen as weak, and would have felt embarrassed if I had to tell my professors that I couldn't complete an assignment because I was feeling too sad that day.

Recently, I have lost touch with several people who I thought were my friends because I realized they weren't empathetic to what I was going through. I think having such a close connection with death has made me realize just how short our time can be, and I don't want to spend time with people who don't value relationships as much.

I haven't been single for more than six months since my dad died. Looking at my relationship that lasted from the end of my freshman year to the beginning of my junior year, I can see that it was not a healthy relationship. I relied on my boyfriend for a lot of emotional support, but would get angry when he couldn't understand the pain I felt. In my current relationship, the subject of my dad and my grief experience is a frequent topic of conversation. He knows the kinds of questions to ask and is patient enough to listen when I need it or to just let me cry into his shoulder if that's what I need. His experiences with the deaths of his aunt and grandfather help him understand what I'm going through. We have made a mutual effort to be there for each other whenever we need it. This relationship is much healthier because he is more of an equal partner than an emotional crutch.

I became involved with a support network for grieving students at the end of my sophomore year, though meetings did not begin until my junior year. I was unfamiliar with support groups and really had no idea what to expect. I was pleasantly surprised, and as a result of my experience with those group meetings, I became an advocate for others who were grieving. I participated in a social media campaign on my Facebook page and openly admitted my loss to all of my Facebook friends to spread the word about student grief, and I started working with children at grief camps to try and help others in a way I felt I hadn't been helped.

Once I realized that grief and all the thoughts, emotions, feelings that can go with it were normal—including guilt and shame—I was able to open up about it. The moment that I stopped treating the death of my dad as a secret was a turning point in my life. I had worried so much about being defined as "the girl with the dead dad" that I suppressed my grief and made it harder on myself. Once I was able to open up about my experience and share the reality of my life with other people, I felt much healthier in many aspects of my life, including my relationships with friends, family, and boyfriend. One positive change from my loss was a greater appreciation of the emotions of others. My experience and recognition of the way I began to heal through expressing my emotions have given me greater patience and understanding while listening to others' expressions of pain.

Going through school for the last four years has been difficult. There are so many things I know now that I wish I had known four years ago, especially about the benefit of taking a gap year to sort through the tough stuff that goes along with grief. I find strength when I think about the person I have become as a result of my struggle, and take pride in the fact that others can rely on me during their times of difficulty.

It had been my dream to come to Northwestern ever since my dad and I visited when I was in seventh grade. We had many conversations about coming to Northwestern and what an amazing opportunity it was going to be. I take solace in the fact that he would be proud of the woman I have become. I try to honor his memory by working as hard as I possibly can to be successful and to pay tribute to all of the sacrifices he made in order to send me to school here.

I will graduate in 16 days, and I would give everything I have if it meant that he could see me walk across that stage. I wish he could see what I've accomplished and celebrate this incredibly important occasion with me. Even though I have avoided thinking about celebrating graduation without him, I know I will need to think through how to approach this moment. I was lucky enough to have the opportunity to choose Northwestern with him, but the idea of starting a new chapter of my life where he is not there to help with my decisions is terrifying. I have learned a lot about myself over the last four years and circumstances made me grow up a lot faster than I ever thought I would. I miss my dad every single day, but I hope that by sharing my story and experiences with other people I can honor his memory and share the strength that he taught me with others.

Questions for Reflection

Please reflect on and/or write out answers to the following questions:

1. What lessons about life, if any, did you learn from your loved one who died and/or from your grieving process? How have these lessons changed your outlook on life?

2. What, if anything, have you learned about friendship?

3. In what ways, if any, have your life priorities shifted?

For supporters:

> What can you do to remain sensitive when grieving students and young adults express possible life lessons connected to their grief? How can you follow their lead and communicate your openness to discussing this topic with them?

CHAPTER 10

Powerful and/or Challenging Grief Reactions

Grievers of all ages can experience diverse and powerful reactions. We knew that the contributing authors would share feelings of shock, anger, guilt, and sadness, but we were not expecting the narratives to describe such intensity. Although these experiences are not unique to college students and young adult grievers, there seemed to be unique developmental features in how they described these responses.

One of the most common emotions described by the students was shock (e.g., unreality, disbelief, and dissociation) at the time of diagnosis and/or upon hearing about the death. Many offered bodily metaphors to express the extent of this experience, such as: "I'd been stabbed," "pit formed in stomach," and "hit me like a ton of bricks." A few students shared powerful feelings of anger connected with their grief experience, generally associated with the unsupportive actions of others. In addition, they often expressed guilt in connection with their anger or in connection with their inability to do more for their loved one who died and/or for their other family members. As expected, sadness was reported by almost all authors. We chose to include this chapter to highlight and demonstrate the many "normal" though intense responses that young adults may experience when grieving.

We have included the following three stories that we believe illustrate the broad range and intensity of the grief reactions of grieving college students and young adults.

Alyssa

Sex: Female

Age: 23

Time since death loss:
3 years, 8 months

During college

Death loss: Father

Heart attack

When I was a sophomore in college, my younger brother called me on a Wednesday afternoon to tell me that our dad had died earlier that day of a heart attack after playing racquetball at the gym. This was April 22, 2009. I was in shock. My dad wasn't sick. He was in perfect health. How could this happen to him?! After the autopsy, we discovered that he had previously had a small heart attack that no one, including my dad, was aware of.

I went straight home from school for a week right after my dad died, and I wasn't able to sleep well. My mom slept with me for the first few nights, but then my aunt said that my mom had to sleep in her own bed again. After that, my best friend from home stayed with me every night. She was especially helpful. She would stay up very late with me watching funny movies until I could fall asleep. Many times during the day, I would randomly start crying because I missed my dad. She would rub my shoulders, listen to me, and she never once was uncomfortable with me being upset. I wrote a eulogy to read at my dad's memorial service. I was worried that I wouldn't be able to read it at the service without breaking down and crying. The day before the memorial service, she listened to me try to read the eulogy until I could get through the entire speech without crying. Her love and support truly helped me get through the most difficult time in my life, and I value my friendship with her so much.

In contrast, one of my other friends from high school came to my dad's memorial service. After the service, everyone came up to my family to give us their condolences. When he came up to me, he said, "Well, at least your dad picked Earth Day to go." I remember being so angry with him for trying to lighten up my father's death. I have since then gotten over this, but it took me a very long time. I know he didn't know what to say and was trying to be helpful, but I would have much preferred him saying he was sorry for my loss and would be there for me as a friend and support.

The main ways I expressed my grief were through anger and sadness. I was angry at the world for being unfair. I was angry that my dad, who was such an amazing and wonderful person, had to die. I was angry because I saw so many toxic, hateful, selfish people in the world still living while my dad was such an empathetic, kind, selfless man and he wasn't living any more. I was angry that I had to grieve his death when he should have been still living and with me. I was sad because I couldn't physically be with my dad anymore. I was sad because I wasn't able to say I love you one last time or say goodbye. I was sad because there was so much that I wanted to learn from my dad that he had not yet taught me, and I don't have the opportunity to learn that wisdom from him.

The first few months after my dad's death were the most difficult. I could be very impatient at times and easily frustrated. I was also sad a lot. It made a big difference when people were not awkward or uncomfortable when I wanted to cry or talk about how I was upset. Even people who weren't very close to me were very supportive. Some people wrote me sympathy cards, which meant a lot to me. Or people would tell me that they were sorry for my loss and that they were here for me if I needed anything from them. This love and support really helped me when I felt low.

I went to counseling and psychological services the first semester after my dad died. This experience was helpful for me. I was able to talk about how much I missed my dad and everything I was going through without feeling like a burden to anyone. It was a free space for me to cry or be angry or feel however I needed to feel at the time. I also learned a lot of great tools to help me cope with my grief. The most helpful tool I learned was to journal every night before going to bed. Journaling has allowed me to express all of the thoughts and feelings racing around in my head that used to keep me from being able to fall asleep.

My college had a student organization that was a support group for grieving students called AMF. This group was so helpful for me because everyone in the group was grieving, like me. We were all able to tell our stories, relate to each other, and give each other support. One of the girls in the group started a program where students who were grieving were matched with a professor. This professor was there to be an additional support for the student. Dr. G was my professor. I met with her once a week until I graduated to talk about whatever I wanted. I loved meeting with Dr. G because she was someone I could trust who was removed from the situation (i.e., she wasn't a family member who was also grieving my dad's death). Her being an adult and not a peer was also very beneficial because she had more wisdom from life, compared to many of my friends. Dr. G was extremely compassionate and empathetic. I remember the first time we met, when I told her about my dad dying and her eyes watered up. I remember thinking *thank you for understanding how I feel!* I felt safe talking to Dr. G about everything I was dealing with in life, and she gave me excellent advice for many of the problems I was going through. I am now a year and a half out of college, but Dr. G and I still keep in touch via phone about once a month.

I have gotten over my anger for the most part. I realize that there are lots of unfair things in the world, and I was lucky to have my dad as my father and not someone else who would have been less compassionate. I realize that I would definitely choose to have *my* dad alive for the short time we had together over any other dad alive for a longer time. I am still sad sometimes, but I have accepted my sadness as a reminder of how much I love my father and the great impact he had on my life. I like to think that it is better to feel sadness about missing my dad than to feel nothing at all.

I now am able to grieve in a more positive way sometimes as well. I enjoy saying jokes and little phrases that I remember my dad used to say all the time. They help me remember him, and this makes me happy. I also try to "live through him." What I mean by this is there are many characteristics that my dad possessed that I look up to, and I try to possess these characteristics as well. Whenever I catch myself acting in a way that my dad used to, it brings a warm feeling to my heart. I feel good knowing that the memory of my dad lives on in me.

Mary

Sex: Female

Age: 23

Time since death loss:
4 years, 9 months

During college

Death loss: Mother

Metastatic breast cancer

My mother passed away 11 days after the end of my first year of college from metastatic breast cancer. She had been ill since I was ten years old.

Initially, I had poor techniques of dealing with my grief. The semester after my mom passed away I signed up for 18 credit hours just to keep myself occupied. I also often drank on the weekends to the point where I would make poor decisions or become very upset. I began to experience insomnia and had constant feelings of worry.

I had people who were there for me and others who just weren't. My dad and brother were by far the best resource I had through that time. They were there for me to talk to when I was unable to be in a room by myself without crying. My friends were as supportive as they could be without fully understanding what I was going through. They kept me company, especially on bad days. For instance, my roommate took the day off on the anniversary of my mom's passing and spent the day with me, doing things that made me think of my mom in a positive way, like going to the mall and trying on the ugliest dresses we could, something my mom and I used to do.

I began a relationship with a guy my age about a year and a half after my mom passed. Looking back, I know that I stayed in that relationship only so that I would not be alone. While he would comfort me when I got upset, he really had no idea what to say to me and often would get frustrated with me on my bad days when I did not want to get out of bed. He did not understand why I wanted so much stability in my personal relationships. I had one friend whose parents had gotten divorced years earlier, and I heard her comparing her experience to mine, saying that she never got upset about her family. This was very difficult for me as she had no clue what it is like to lose a parent.

In my junior year of school I reached a point where I felt like I had hit rock bottom and would never feel hopeful again. At that point, with the support of my friends and family, I decided to see a counselor. I had begun to feel like I did not want to do anything at all. I remember not wanting to spend time with my friends and there were days that I did not even want to get out of bed. Finally, before entering graduate school, I decided to go on antidepressants to help me in dealing with my feelings of indifference, fatigue, and depression. Counseling was a godsend. It took some time to become comfortable with a counselor, but it ended up being very beneficial in the end. I remember the day in counseling when I was able to say "my mom" and talk about the positive things I remembered about her, instead of referring to her only as "she" or "her" and my memories being clouded by all the pain, suffering, and constant worry.

There came a point during graduate school when I finally felt like myself again. I was happy, energetic, laughing, and loving what I was doing and I had no guilt about these feelings. I had reached the point where I was able to accept being happy because I knew my mom would want this. I was able to wean off the medication and stop seeing counselors. Currently, I am working in my dream job after receiving my degree, something my mom and I had dreamed of since I was 14. As hard as those years were, I think going through them made me the person I am now. And I think my mom would be proud of who I am now.

Loreal

Sex: Female

Age: 21

Time since death loss:
4 years, 6 months

Prior to college

Death loss: Mother

Diving accident

My mom passed away due to a snorkeling accident the summer before I started college. I felt that my whole life had fallen apart. I felt so lost. I was raised to be a very independent person so, before my mom died, moving more than 200 miles away to college seemed like such a long-awaited adventure. Now, the thought of going to college seemed like such a scary and uncertain experience. Luckily, my sisters decided to help me to the best of their abilities as I started school. Still, neither one of them could replace the role my mom had in my life. I also felt cheated because they had our mom to help them with the "college transition." That feeling of emptiness became ever present throughout my first year of college.

That was when I began to hide the fact that my mom had died. Anytime someone I met would talk about their parents or ask me about mine, I would go on talking as if my mom was still alive. I only let a handful of people know she had died and what I was going through. With the people I did tell, a version of the phrase, "I'm sorry to hear that" would be used. The phrase, though it was intended to be consoling, conveyed a feeling of discomfort with the subject, and led me to be very cautious about whom I divulged my loss to. I was truly afraid of making people uncomfortable or having to retell the story of how she died. In many ways, I felt my life was not my own and I was having a hard time grasping the reality that was now my life.

Balancing the changes in my family life and those in my new college life was an ongoing struggle. I was trying to deal with my grief, and make it through my first year of college like any average freshman. I never told my professors and knew little about what was available to me to help me with my grief. In addition, the stigma of going to a professional counselor made me wary of utilizing the student wellness center. The main way I coped my freshman year was to constantly avoid the topic of my grief in public and to only express it in private.

Friends of mine from high school, who knew my mom had died, did their best to keep me from becoming a recluse and would ask me to spend time with them. It was a comfort to have these friends, but none of them knew what it was like to grieve, and being with them became another way to avoid my grief. We rarely talked about my mom, and I did not have the courage to bring up the topic at the time. There were many instances where my friends would complain about how their moms were being overly protective by calling too much. I wished my mom was calling me "too much."

The longing to meet another college student who knew what it felt like to lose a loved one became a constant thought for me. With that yearning, I took a chance and attended a peer-led grief support group meeting at the student wellness center, and I met a student who had lost her stepfather a few months before. We bonded almost instantly through our losses and I told her about my attempt to start a local chapter of a peer network for grieving students on our campus. She was immediately interested and became the co-leader of the group. She was the first person I met who had experienced a loss in college. Our constant communication and work together began to alleviate my feelings of loneliness. The sense of mutual understanding of grief between us made such a huge difference in my life, like nothing else before had.

My Catholic faith was another comforting factor throughout my college years. I attended church regularly from a very young age, and, during college, I met strong and nurturing individuals at St. Augustine church who had gone through many similar life experiences. During the fall of my sophomore year, one of my friends suggested I attend the church's semesterly college retreat with her. I was uncertain about attending, but the retreat quickly became another avenue for me to acknowledge the death of my mom. Many of the attendees talked about their own grief experiences, which made me want to share the story of my faith journey through my loss. When I did so, many of my peers felt a strong connection with my story, and I felt like I had come to a new phase in my grief journey.

With both the establishment of the local grief support network and my connection with other students involved with St. Augustine, I came to terms with the idea that it was OK to share my grief with others. Gradually, I felt more comfortable and realized that through sharing I could help other students who, like me, felt alone in their losses. Compartmentalizing my grief and not sharing my story was a disservice to other students who were likely going through similar emotions, but were apprehensive to share.

My emotions can still go up and down. At any moment, tears can begin to well up at the thought that my mom cannot physically be in my life anymore. Fortunately, most days, I think of my mom with fond reverence and love.

I distinctly remember the day before I graduated college. All of my friends were with their families, but I was alone in my room crying. It was the first time my mom would not be at my graduation. From kindergarten to high school, she was the one who bought me flowers and inspired me to work hard, to be a leader, and to persevere against the odds, so it was devastating not to have her there. As the sadness overwhelmed me, my roommate knocked on my door to ask me a question. She saw the tears coming down my face and just gave me a hug. She had no idea what I was going through, but to have her at least try to console me made me feel a bit better. The day of my graduation, all of my closest friends from college were there even though I had not invited them to be there. That was exactly what I needed. I did my best to hide my sadness that day. No one knew what I was feeling at the time, but a hug and a few texts from my loved ones telling me how proud they were of me made all the difference.

Over the years, my grief story has taken on many chapters. The most important lessons that I have learned are to appreciate the times you had with your loved ones and to remember that you are not alone. There are so many people in this world going through the loss of a loved one and even though each grief story is different, we all share that one common bond. Also, my losses actually provide me with an important way to help others who are grieving.

Questions for Reflection

Please reflect on and/or write out answers to the following questions:

1. What were your primary reactions after your loved one died? Which reactions concerned you the most? Which reactions remain the most powerful for you?

2. How did you cope with your most powerful grief reactions? As you look back, what other coping approaches do you believe could have been helpful?

3. If someone shared with you that he or she recently lost a loved one, how would you respond? What words or actions would you choose? What coping approaches might you suggest to someone who is experiencing intense grief reactions, such as shock, anger, guilt, and/or sadness?

For supporters:

> What powerful and/or challenging reactions have you observed in the grieving college students and young adults you seek to support? What were some of the ways you assisted them in coping with these reactions? What new approaches to assisting them could you consider using in the future?

CHAPTER 11

Importance of a
Community of Support

Just as support from a grieving peer or a mentor can be extremely helpful, it appears that support from each additional community member can be additive and even synergistic. Receiving support from multiple sources can be particularly helpful for grievers. All of our authors addressed the importance of support; they received different types of support (e.g., tangible, emotional, distraction) from a number of important others including friends who knew their loved one and those who did not, immediate and extended family members, mentors, professors, and sometimes even strangers.

Most of the authors in this book did not experience support from multiple sources, but we did want to highlight those students who did. The authors below described receiving support from an entire track team, a student-led grief organization, and a variety of supporters within a small school.

A few of our authors (not all in this chapter) also experienced challenging breaches of support from within their communities. They described the ending of friendships and minimizing messages that seemed to contribute to the authors questioning the validity of their own grief experiences. Grief had "weeded out" those who could not be supportive, and they learned to move toward those who wanted to help.

We have included the following three stories that we believe illustrate the importance of a community of support in the lives of grieving college students and young adults.

Isabel

Sex: Female

Age: 24

Time since death loss: 3 years, 11 months

During college

Death loss: Father

Hemorrhagic stroke

My dad died on November 10, 2008 from a severe hemorrhagic stroke. I was three weeks into my junior year of college, and my first term at a new school, when I got a phone call that changed my life. I was volunteering to be a "conversation partner" for international students and was at the opening event when I got a phone call from my mom. I hit the ignore button, assuming that since they were coming to visit the next day it was just details on when they would be arriving. I was wrong. She was calling because my dad had had a stroke and was on his way to the hospital. I went back and forth between school and home for three-and-a-half weeks before my dad was taken off of life support. He died three days later.

I was numb for the first two months. I went back to school a week after my dad died, but it felt like I was sleepwalking through life. I do not remember the end of that term or the first few weeks of the winter quarter. I kept thinking about the things that my dad would miss. I cried a lot, not when I was in class, but when I was alone in my apartment. To this day, I am still mad at myself for not being there when he died. My sisters and I had gone home for the night (dad was in the hospital) because we thought we could not handle what we knew was coming.

I had solid support from a number of people in my life. The most supportive people, in my opinion, were my roommates. Throughout the entire ordeal, they stuck by my side and made sure that I wasn't fixating on my loss. They showed their support by finding activities for us to do together that would allow me to have fun and get my mind off my grief, even if only temporarily. One of my roommates had lost her mom to cancer when she was younger, so she understood what I was going through. When I went home each weekend, she would email to check in on me and when I was at school, she would always be there to talk or go out to dinner or go shopping. When I got the phone call from my sister saying that they were taking my dad off life support she sat with me until my mom arrived. She supported me when I was away for a week and when I got back. I can't say how much I appreciated her support. The faculty members at my campus were very understanding and pledged to help me get through the end of the term any way that they could. I am happy to say that they carried out their pledge by giving me extra time to complete my work and allowing me to take tests that I would have otherwise missed. My family was very supportive, but was also grieving.

My friends from high school, who actually knew my dad, were not supportive to me. They did not speak to me about my dad's death, or they would try to relate to my grief by talking about how a grandparent or pet had died. One of my friends from high school called me to talk after my dad died. She kept turning the conversation back to her and trying to relate by talking about how her grandparent, who she normally spoke poorly of, had died. She just couldn't get it. I appreciated the effort, but it really made me feel like no one I had grown up with cared about my loss. The people who I had met at school only weeks before were much more supportive than anyone I grew up with.

At school, I connected with the local chapter of a support network for grieving students. My friends in the chapter were able to relate to what I was going through, even though they all had different losses. We came together to have coffee, go to movies, and talk outside of our meetings. The group gave me a place where I didn't feel judged for my grief. No one gave me pitying looks and the others knew what to do to not make me feel uncomfortable.

Bethany

Sex: Female

Age: 28

Time since death loss: 6 years

During college

Death loss: Mother

Ovarian cancer

My mom passed away on November 19, 2006 from ovarian cancer after a five-and-half year battle. I was a college sophomore at the time. I attended college four hours away from home and by the time my dad realized how seriously ill my mom was at the end, she was already in a coma. I never got to say goodbye to her.

I returned to college a week after my mom's death. I was overwhelmed, angry, and extremely devastated. I had no idea how I was supposed to move forward from my loss; just the thought of "moving on" was so overwhelming I felt paralyzed with grief. I am a religious person (Christian) so I was also angry at God for taking my mom away from me. My mom and I were extremely close. My sadness felt all consuming. I went on auto-drive; I was trying survive school, extracurricular activities (I was a residential assistant), and my job as a student admissions counselor.

After the initial six weeks of shock, I was overwhelmed with so much sadness and grief, my dad was concerned I was becoming depressed and urged me to get counseling. I followed my dad's advice. During the spring semester, I did go to counseling. Counseling helped give me permission to accept my grief, embrace it, but also learn how to move forward.

I was fortunate to have people who were there for me. My dad was extremely supportive of me; he was always available to listen and encourage me. Despite my dad's distance, he was always a phone call away. My mentor also regularly stopped by my dorm to check on me and somehow knew the balance of pushing me forward, but not letting me give up or quit. That accountability and care was instrumental as I maneuvered through my new normal.

My friends were extremely wonderful. One of my roommates let me cry and process my grief in our room. She never complained about my odd hours, sometimes I would stay up until 2 or 4 in the morning unable to sleep because I was grieving. Another friend provided a refuge for many years on Mother's Day, which is a day I have had a particularly hard time with. She also has never forgotten that each "big" event in my life (e.g., graduation, engagement, marriage, birth of my child) would be mixed with sadness too. My remaining friends would check on me regularly and were always willing to talk and listen to how I was doing. Their availability was incredible. Faculty members and extended family members were also very supportive. The admissions office where I worked was tremendous. The staff attended my mom's funeral and they remained supportive. Residential life was monumental. They were so supportive and helpful.

Peers, such as classmates who I was not close to, were the ones who showed a lack of understanding. I often got comments such as, "What is going on with you? You are acting weird." I learned that they weren't trying to be hurtful; my loss seemed so distant to them, even though it was still so fresh to me. Those comments, combined with my grief, provided me with a deeper level of compassion that I didn't have before I lost my mom. It made me realize that all people go through a loss of some type, and that one loss is not greater than another. It is still loss and loss is uncomfortable for everyone.

Jeffrey

Sex: Male

Age: 26

Time since death loss:
5 years, 9 months

During college

Death loss: Father

Car accident

I remember exactly when I got the phone call that changed my life forever: Friday, April 20, 2007. I was asleep, having gone to bed earlier than usual, to prepare for a track meet the following day. My older brother, Tim, called me, crying, "He's gone, Jeff. Dad died." As I had just woken up from a deep sleep, it took me a while to process what my brother had said. I felt like I had the wind knocked out of me—my father was gone. He was driving home late at night, lost control and collided with a telephone pole, immediately dying from blunt force trauma.

I called my mother quickly after. When I was growing up as a kid, I always pictured us as a perfect family, where nothing went wrong and nothing bad seemed to happen. Even as a 20-year-old college student, I continued to call my mom for advice or when I just wanted to hear her say, "Everything's going to be all right." But when I called her the night of my father's death, I could tell my tough, resilient mother had been broken. She not only lost the father of her three boys, but her husband of 26 years (their anniversary was the night before), her companion, and her best friend. As I talked to her on the phone, I wanted her to say, "Everything's going to be all right," but I knew that she would not be able to tell me that this time.

I wanted to drive home immediately, but since I went to college in Baltimore, I was nearly 300 miles away from our home in Connecticut. I tried to fall asleep before taking a train early the next morning, but millions of thoughts were racing through my head: *What was the last thing we talked about? What was the last thing I said to him? Was I mad for some ridiculous foolish reason?* In the morning, I told my roommates what happened and called my coach to tell him I would not be making the bus. He responded that my team, my second family, would be there for me for anything. When I got off the train in New Haven, my father's good friend, who had actually been with him the night that he died, met me at the station.

When we arrived home in Cheshire, I walked into to a room full of family and friends. But I remember not even noticing them and scanning the crowd for my mother's face. I saw a bunch of people gathered on the porch, and I had a flashback to when my grandfather passed away. I was probably only eight years old, but I remember my parents and my uncles gathered on the porch, discussing funeral arrangements with the priest and the funeral home director. When I saw her and our eyes connected, I completely broke down. My mother is the strongest person I know, and I could not imagine what she must have been feeling.

The rest of the weekend seemed like a blur, but I distinctly remember the outpouring of support from family and friends. We live in a small suburban town in Connecticut, but I remember traffic being backed up for miles as people waited to offer their condolences at my father's wake. More than ten of my track friends drove up from Baltimore for less than two hours just to give me a hug. All of these people that came to support us helped me with the initial grief. One thing that has helped since are the phone calls from close friends on the anniversary just to let me know that they are thinking about me.

I think it is hard for anyone to truly "get" what you are going through when a tragic event like this happens. Some may have lost a family member to cancer or to another disease, but when you lose someone unexpectedly, you never get to say goodbye. There is no way to gradually prepare yourself for either the finality or the magnitude of the loss. Through the peer-led support groups I have attended, I have been able to talk about my grief and express what I would have said to my father had I had the opportunity. Furthermore, nearly one year after my father unexpectedly passed, a close friend of mine lost his father to a heart attack. Even though I had been through nearly the same type of loss, I felt at a loss for words when I called him. Sometimes there really is nothing you can say, but you can be there for the person if they want to talk.

In the years following my father's death, I occasionally find it hard to talk about him, but I also take solace in knowing that part of him lives on through my brothers and me. His humor, his hardworking nature, his dedication to family, and, as my brother recently said during a speech at my wedding, his gray hair.

Questions for Reflection

Please reflect on and/or write out answers to the following questions:

1. Who were/are those most supportive people in your grief journey? How did/do they show their support?

2. Who were/are the least supportive in your grief? How did they show their lack of support?

3. What was a unique or interesting act of support that surprised you?

4. If you are a college student, think about the resources that your campus offers. In what ways does your college handle grief well? In what areas could they improve?

For supporters:

Do the grieving college students and young adults you seek to support have a community of supporters to turn to? What are some things that you can do to enhance the supportiveness of their community?

CHAPTER 12

Changing Family Relationships

The illness or death of a family member can seriously shake up family dynamics (Walsh and McGoldrick, 2004). The family is no longer the same as it was before and although it seems as if everyone "should" be grieving the same (because they lost the same person), grief is actually unique not only because of who we are as people, but also because of the unique relationship we had with the person who died. No two family members experienced the death of the same relationship. The authors definitely reflected on this idea of distinct grief.

They also focused on shifting roles within their families, both for themselves and for their remaining parents and/or siblings. When a family member dies, others often attempt to fill in the roles that person played (e.g., glue, joker, stabilizer) and/or the family has to find new ways of functioning without those roles. The authors often described a hole in their own life and in the life of their family—and that part of grieving and mourning was finding ways to fill that hole.

A few authors identified challenges with feeling alone within their family because of differences in grief expression. In many cases, these differences were connected with some perceived judgment of each other's experiences (i.e., how one should grieve) and an inability to offer support to one another. However, some students expressed understanding of the unique personalities of their family members and their unique relationships with the deceased, allowing for more tolerance and understanding of differential expressions of grief.

New romantic relationships for surviving parents can be particularly challenging for children of a recently deceased parent. There are norms related to how long someone "should" wait to date or remarry after the death of a spouse; feelings of anger and confusion can follow when these norms are not followed.

We have included the following two stories that we believe illustrate the shifting nature of family relationships in the lives of grieving college students and young adults.

Meghan Rizon

Sex: Female

Age: 21

Time since death loss: 3 years, 1 month

Prior to college

Death loss: Mother

Breast cancer

When I was 18, my mother died of breast cancer that had metastasized to her brain. She was sick for a really long time before she died; she was originally diagnosed when I was ten years old. Soon after her diagnosis, my father moved to another state, and I ceased having a relationship with him.

Being the oldest, I felt it was my responsibility to help Mom with her illness; I helped her through chemotherapy, radiation, complementary and alternative therapies, and periods of remission. When I was 16, I spent the entire summer as her caregiver at the Cancer Treatment Center of America. Not even two years later, the cancer had metastasized to her brain, and she started to decline. She quickly lost motor and mental function, and we had to place her in a nursing home where she continued to receive palliative care until she died in hospice. Cancer isn't just a disease that metastasizes in the body—it also metastasizes in every other aspect of life. It gradually takes away more and more, and you keep fighting and fighting it, until eventually you become a person you don't even recognize anymore. It is a rollercoaster ride of loss, change, and adaptation, and you live your whole life trying to stay one step ahead of a disease that has the capability to take away everything from you.

The year she died, I was a senior in high school. It was a time of intense pressure and stress, both academically and personally. In every way possible, that year was one of incredible transitions— life to death, high school to college, and teenager to young adult. If I wasn't studying, then I was at the hospital or nursing home or chemo; often I was studying even while there. A few weeks after her death my college tuition deposit was due. I remember being on the phone with all of my potential universities, asking for extensions on the deposit, because my mom had just died, and I hadn't even had time to choose a school. As a graduating senior, everybody expected so much from me, but the one thing nobody seemed to expect was that I would need a break. I kept that stress inside me—I didn't allow myself to feel the loss. I did all the post-graduation stuff that I thought I was supposed to do, but the whole time, I never acknowledged my grief.

Everyone acted as if she had never existed. Nobody ever talked about her. I felt as if nobody understood what I was going through. More importantly, it seemed there was nobody who *wanted* to understand. I always felt that by talking about it, I would be making *other people* feel uncomfortable. So I didn't. But I yearned for someone to say something about Mom—to acknowledge that she was here, that she existed. I wanted to feel like I wasn't the only one who missed her, but nobody ever talked about her, not even my grandparents.

When summer finally arrived, I had something new to focus on: Mom's estate. My grandmother, who I thought I could trust, ended up denying me the right to participate in enacting Mom's last wishes. Things that she explicitly told me she wanted me to do, I was prevented from doing. I felt betrayed, stressed, angry, and I felt like I was letting Mom down. I was so involved in her care while she was sick, that I just assumed I would be equally as involved after her death. But my grandmother refused to include me in the organizing of the estate.

Eventually, I started noticing physical symptoms. Toward the end of the summer I became very tired and fatigued. Mentally, I seemed the same, but my body was very weak. I would spend the day on the couch, watching TV, because I didn't have the energy to do anything else. That happened occasionally, so I didn't think too much of it. But then it started happening more frequently, and it got to the point where I would be fatigued for weeks. I never once associated the fatigue with grief or any other feelings.

Then, I was off to college. But literally the second I stepped onto campus, I started grieving. In that moment, all I could see were kids with their parents, and I felt Mom's absence so acutely—like a bullet to the heart. It was and is a pain that I will never be able to completely describe in words. When I got to college, my life became completely about me. No ailing mother to look after, no siblings to drive to school, no groceries to shop for—everything was about me. The problem was I did not know who I was without her, without cancer, and without all of my responsibilities that seemed to have died right along with her. I experienced intense feelings of isolation—I felt I was not able to relate to my peers because I wasn't able to focus on school, I didn't want to go out and socialize, I had no family back home that I could talk to, and I didn't know how to convey my feelings to myself, let alone to other people. I started feeling fatigued all the time.

Eventually, I sought out help. From the time Mom was diagnosed until I called the university's psychological services, I was always adamantly against counseling or therapy. I believed I needed to deal with it on my own—that it was my burden to bear. However, once I started college, the grief became very intense. It scared me. I was always fatigued, and I had no energy to participate in college life. I had trouble concentrating, and I had lost my motivation to study. These were extreme behavioral changes, and they prompted me to seek help. Soon after I started counseling, I also discovered a peer-led support group for grieving students. As I met other students and started talking more in counseling, I became less reserved about my feelings. I cannot stress enough how valuable counseling and the support group have been. They've helped me separate myself from the loss. I created my own support system and, by doing this, I put myself on a path to healing that I believe I am still walking.

My mom always said, "Expand your horizons," but it wasn't until after she died that I could truly start living by that philosophy. Before her death, I was always a "caregiver" or a "student," but after her death, I saw myself as nothing. I saw myself as purposeless, useless—if I couldn't help my mom through cancer then what was I supposed to do? So I had to expand my horizons in a very intrapersonal way. I had to break away from those definitions of myself, and most importantly, I had to finally start feeling my loss. I had to say goodbye to the mother who was healthy, goodbye to the mother who died, and goodbye to the mother that I would never have in the future. I had to feel emotions I had never let myself feel before—sadness, anger, depression—I had to process them, and I had to seek out support from others. In this way, I had expanded the horizons within myself. I wish my mother had never died. I wish she had never gotten sick. But I am so grateful for the lessons she has taught me after death. For helping me, as she did in life, become the best person that I can be.

Na Hyung

Sex: Female

Age: 22

Time since death loss: 4 years, 1 month

Prior to college

Death loss: Mother

Cancer

I lost my mother to cancer at age 18, in my last semester of high school. Despite the relatively sudden loss, I was able to finish my year successfully and enjoyably because of the support from my friends and teachers. However, when I came to college, I lost that support base and found it hard to relate to other freshmen. I often felt the need to share about my loss, but I hesitated because I didn't want to be judged, pitied, or simply to make a conversation awkward. As a result it was hard to build new friendships. At the same time, I had to care for my younger brother and father, who were struggling on their own at home.

An important way that my grief has been and is expressed is through dreaming. I seem to think about my mother the most in my subconscious when I am asleep. Every time I have such a dream and wake up, I like to lie in my bed and replay my interaction (or non-interaction) with my mother in that dream. Often I will write about it.

Here is a blog post I wrote in December 2012 that illustrates my typical "grief expression":

Funny thing, loss…

I do not often break down and cry about it. But when I do, I often surprise myself. I do not need to be distressed for it to happen. It's not mood-dependent—what kind of a day, week, or month I'm having. Rather, it takes a trigger at a peaceful hour.

Tonight, the trigger was a voice recording from Thanksgiving Day: my dad singing and playing "See you in the sad season" by Baek Young-Kyu. The oldies melody led me on a journey through YouTube searching out every Korean song from the 70s and the 80s. Next thing I know, I was digging for the specific oldies songs my mom used to enjoy. I couldn't get enough of the warm fuzziness those songs gave me. When I finally decided I should go to sleep, I suddenly found myself in tears.

I go through my days, walking through all the streets my mom has never walked on, driving a car she never rode in, doing things she never saw me do, working toward goals she never would have expected, seeing people she never met… There is not much room in my head to make connections between Mom and what I am doing during the day. That's why, late at night, by myself without much stress or outside distraction, stripped to the heart of my heart, I come back to her. And the tears and longing take me by surprise. I realized tonight that I'm like a little kid. I'm almost twenty-two and multiple times a year I still cry, "I want my mommy…"

I think these things that take you by surprise are what lie in the deepest parts of your heart. Something you don't normally think about in the midst of busyness but do keep coming back to whenever you're removed from it all. People you long for, issues that need to be addressed…

Although I no longer feel alienated or misunderstood because of my loss, I know I need to deal with other issues stemming from it. For example, my religious views changed in college. I think that transitioning away from Christianity to another form of spirituality would have been much simpler if I had not promised to my mother on her deathbed that I would always communicate with her through prayers. The main way I coped with my loss was holding the religious beliefs that my mother held (e.g., it's OK because we will see each other again in Heaven), so the gradual fading and transitioning of my faith have been especially difficult. It's something I am still working through, and talking with other grieving students has been invaluable for learning how people from different cultural backgrounds deal with death and possible afterlife.

Several months into college, I was fortunate enough to come across a peer-led support group for grieving students. Being involved in this organization and volunteering for a local hospice helped me to channel my grief toward helping others and to open up to others about my loss. Those who have also lost a parent or a sibling at a "young age" just understand. With those people, simply letting me know that they also had that experience comforted me more than anything anyone could do. Also, people who have gone through other unusually difficult life experiences (e.g., illness, sexual abuse), either first-hand or second-hand, seem to "get it" relatively well. I could talk with these people about my loss and grief easily because we knew that we suffered from something that we did not normally talk to others about.

February is a difficult month for me because February 5, 2009 was when my mother was put in the ICU with a respirator, February 7 was her birthday with her in a coma, February 12 was when she died, and February 14 (Valentine's Day) was her memorial service. A friend knew this and surprised me with lilies (my and my mother's favorite flower) and a hand-made card on the first anniversary of her death. He was never too shy to bring my mother up in a thoughtful conversation and always patiently listening when I had something to say about her. Last February, an unexpected email from this friend, asking if I was doing OK that month and letting me know he was still thinking about her, made everything better.

My relationships within my family have been more challenging. Unfortunately, I do not talk with my brother about my mother as much as I would like to because he is introverted and I cannot tell if he wants to. But the few times that we will mention a memory of her and smile/laugh about it together mean the world to me. It's also been tough dealing with my father's remarriage. Overall, my father and I have an extremely good relationship, and we love each other to pieces (and show it). But his way of coping, for a year or two after my mother's death, was to try to not think or talk about her at all. This is the opposite of how I have been coping. Especially since he got remarried and I now have a stepmother and stepbrothers, there is no opportunity to reminisce about my mother or to ask my father questions about her. We never talk about my childhood (meaning ages 0–18) any more. I am glad he has found a way to cope, but while he can find a new wife, I cannot find a new mother.

One particular difficult time with my father was Mother's Day a couple years ago. My father urged me to wish my new stepmother a happy Mother's Day, so I sent her a text message. He got upset with me because I did not give her a call. I got upset because I was preoccupied and somewhat down with thoughts of my mother that day as I am every year. He did not seem sensitive to that possibility at all. We had a talk, and we have been more considerate toward each other on holidays since then. It's been very difficult to be unable to talk about my childhood and my mother with the single person in the world who knows both the best. I hope that eventually my father will be able to soften and open up a bit because I have so many questions to ask about my mother, but I have to keep in mind that he is also, in his own way, grieving.

Questions for Reflection

Please reflect on and/or write out answers to the following questions:

1. How did your family change after your loved one died? How did you cope with these changes?

2. What were similarities and differences between how you and other members of your family expressed your grief? How did you cope with any differences?

3. What were similarities and differences between how you and other members of your family wanted to remember your loved one who died? How did you cope with any differences?

4. What could/can you say to loved ones who may be coping differently from you, to help you both in understanding and accepting your differences?

For supporters:

What changes have you observed in the families of the grieving college students and young adults you are seeking to support? What could you say and/or do to help them in coping with these changing family relationships?

CHAPTER 13

Tips for Grieving College Students and Young Adults

Now that you have read 33 narratives by grieving young adults and answered questions related to your personal grief journey, we want you to have a toolkit of tips to help you with integrating these ideas as you move forward in your own grief journey. In this chapter, we offer tips for grieving college students and young adults; each of these tips comes directly from the authors who contributed to this book.

We provide a brief description of each suggestion followed by quote(s) that help illustrate the "lived" experience of each of these ideas. Although a few of these quotes are repeated from the stories included in other chapters, the majority do not appear anywhere else in the book. These suggestions are not meant to be prescriptions for how to grieve correctly, rather they are possible ideas to consider as part of your toolkit. Some of these suggestions were reported by many, whereas others were only noted by a few. Please view these ideas as possibilities and be sure to personally evaluate how well each may or may not fit for you.

For Grieving College Students and Young Adults

> Find personally meaningful ways to memorialize your loved one(s) who died. There can be many seemingly small and routine but personally important ways to remember and honor your loved one(s).

"I wear my dad's wedding chain on his birthday and his death anniversary as a display of honoring his memory and hoping to get people to ask about him, so I can tell his story."

"I enjoy saying jokes and little phrases that I remember my dad used to say all the time. They help me remember him, and this makes me happy. I also try to 'live through him.' What I mean by this is there are many characteristics that my dad possessed that I look up to, and I try to possess these characteristics as well."

Be kind and patient with yourself in terms of commitments, demands, and choices about how to spend your time. Allow yourself plenty of time to do normal everyday activities. Try not to over-schedule yourself, because you don't need the added stress. Rest when you can and need to; it's not a sign of weakness.

"I came back to school less than a month after my brother died and, second only to taking care of myself, my priority was to try to graduate. Because of that, I largely did not become involved in many of the campus activities that I had had leadership positions in, in the past."

"Unlike my peers, I was not so stressed out thinking that school was the be all and end all and I needed to focus only on it... I wanted to graduate, which I did, and I enjoyed my courses, but at the same time I did not care about school at all in some ways, because my mind was with my brother and my main focus was taking care of myself."

"In general, my tolerance for things I did not really enjoy went way way down, and I don't think that is entirely or even mostly a bad thing. Certainly, it was hard to deal with if I couldn't change my circumstances, but when I could, I became quite decisive and fast-acting."

Work to connect with your grieving family members and yet remember that each member of your family with grieve in his or her own way.

"Treating my mom and sister more 'peer' like—not saying that my mom isn't still my mom, but talking more openly and freely with her—has been really important to me."

"Even family members who were missing him too grieved very differently than me, so although I know we're all hurting it is sometimes incredibly difficult to connect over it, and even hurtful when they react to my grief or do not consider it at all in some ways."

"I now understand that it was never my family's intention to make me feel as though I couldn't turn to them. Rather, their way of dealing with the grief, and experience of losing my mom, was to not dwell on the situation emotionally. So instead of crying, it was best to just accept what was happening and continue living life as normal as possible."

Find and connect with peers who have similar grief experiences. Although it may be challenging to find them, they are out there. Risk sharing about your experience with others and you will find those you can relate to.

"Meeting others who have been through similar things, hearing their stories, and getting the opportunity to share mine has also helped me feel more open and unburdened by my painful experience."

"One person that was particularly helpful and supportive was my friend Angela. Angela and I bonded very quickly, because we have both lost a parent to cancer… I looked to her as a source of inspiration, and knowledge of how to deal with my mom's illness and passing. I know that if I'm ever having a difficult day,

I can always call her, to either vent my frustrations or receive an uplifting quote, or much needed advice. Some of the best advice I've ever received from her is quite simply, 'Take everything one day at a time. If necessary, take it hour by hour.' I live by that mantra, even now."

Seek out and connect with potential mentors in your life.

"It was also a nice group of people (in pottery class off campus), many of whom were older than me and had lost someone before, who often actively checked in to see how I was doing that week when we saw each other in class."

"My supervisor at the time had lost her father when she was young and she comforted me in simple ways: calling to check up on me on days when I wasn't working, inviting me to go hiking so that I could vent my frustrations, and spending her lunch hour with me."

Engage in community service projects. Contributing to causes, including those where you help others who are grieving, can offer a sense of giving back to the world and a feeling of control in an out of control situation.

"Working on projects made me feel that, even though I couldn't control my father's illness or the chaos at home, I could be proactive in some way. Attending the Walk to Defeat ALS each fall was particularly important to me. It allowed me to feel as if I were helping my dad and others who were going through the same thing by raising money and awareness."

"One such place that became a weekly respite for me was Challah for Hunger. It was a nonprofit that began at Scripps, where students baked hundreds of loaves of challah each week, and the proceeds funded humanitarian efforts in Darfur. The loftier mission was inspiring, but I found the simple act of weekly baking had even deeper personal meaning. It got me out of my head, into a kitchen, and surrounded by like-minded friends. Those quiet moments, with only the oven buzzing behind me, made the rest of my world recede for a few hours. And, the routine—kneading dough, watching the braids rise, and providing a weekly treat for everyone on campus—made me feel more connected to my community than anything else."

"It is such a privilege to be there with others during their times of grief, walking with them hand-in-hand through the darkness. This is what I feel I was *meant* to do. My losses certainly changed my life, but changed it for the good by giving me purpose and a sense of direction."

Consider religion, spirituality, and faith as possible sources of comfort and support.

"Before my dad became sick, religion played an important role in my life and after he passed away I often found respite from grief in church."

"I am an active member of a campus ministry called Christian Campus Fellowship. Here, I have finally found my home away from home. I found people that care for me and I am learning ways to heal through getting to know others and myself and believing in God. I see life through different eyes now and I believe that God has a plan for each of us."

"I went to late-night Mass by myself, not so much to pray, but more so to have quiet time to sit and talk to my mom."

Reframe your grief (if and when possible) from something negative to a recognition of your love for the person who died. We grieve in proportion to our love.

"I have transformed into a completely new person. I am proud of who I am today and I know my sister would be very proud as well. There is still the part of me that feels I can do it alone that wants to be 'independent'. But, I know that to heal and truly be strong, I need to face my pain, talk about my feelings and be vulnerable with others… The ironic thing is, through my sister's death, I have learned to *live*."

"At first I was nervous about having 'daddy issues' or 'daddy moments' when I'd cry because of a dad-related emotional trigger, and now I am proud of it as a testament to what I've experienced, his importance, and my growth."

"I am still sad sometimes, but I have accepted my sadness as a reminder of how much I love my father and the great impact he had on my life. I like to think that it is better to feel sadness about missing my dad than to feel nothing at all."

Explore counseling as an option. remember that counselors are people, and you may need to try a couple before you find someone who feels comfortable for you. *Important note: You should consider professional help if you feel overwhelmed, hopeless, or helpless; you must seek help if you have suicidal thoughts. You can also call the National (U.S.) Suicide Prevention Lifeline (24/7) at 1–800–273-TALK (8255) or the Samaritans (U.K.) at 08457 909090.*

"I went to Counseling and Psychological Services the first semester after my dad died. This experience was very helpful for me. I was able to talk about how much I missed my dad and everything I was going through without feeling like a burden to anyone. It was a free space for me to cry or be angry or feel however I needed to feel at the time. I also learned a lot of great tools to help me cope with my grief."

"Counseling was a godsend. It took some time to become comfortable with a counselor but it ended up being very beneficial in the end."

"I followed my dad's advice. During the spring semester, I did go to counseling. Counseling helped give me permission to accept my grief, embrace it, but also learn how to move forward."

Engage in a moderate amount of physical activity and monitor your own sense of when you may use physical outlets as an "escape."

"Another way in which I coped was through running. At times I would bury my grief and emotion so deep that the only way to reach it was to run in the trails around Georgetown until finally my emotion would boil to the surface. I spent many days running alone in those woods, where it was safe to shed a tear without making others uncomfortable or worse, inviting them into the pain I was experiencing."

"One thing I did lean on was working out. I worked out hard and often, and I still do. Working out, lifting weights, running and dancing are very meaningful for me and are a great release."

Realize that not everyone in your life will support you in the same way—different people have different ways of being supportive.

"Depending on who they were, they showed their understanding in whatever ways they knew how. Whether just by making sure to ask about 'your mom' instead of 'your parents,' or bringing us food."

"Different people in my life, and even strangers, were amazingly supportive in a range of ways. Many people, in their own ways, were very supportive."

"The support group was my solace. I was still embarrassed to talk to my non-grieving friends about the group, so I'd make up excuses about why I had to leave to go to support-related meetings or events. I rarely invited my roommates to events and fundraisers. Looking back, this was probably a disservice to the group. But I liked that the two worlds were separate, I didn't want to taint my normal friendships with sadness, pity, and that uncomfortable feeling when no one knows what to say."

Pursue creative expression in ways that may be indirectly or directly related to your loved one(s) who died.

"The most helpful tool I learned was to journal every night before going to bed. Journaling has allowed me to express all of the thoughts and feelings racing around in my head that used to keep me from being able to fall asleep."

"I took a pottery class, and loved reconnecting with my passion for ceramics, being able to do something even when I couldn't focus enough for academic work, and working on a long-term project to honor my brother."

"The experience grounded me, gave my grief a purpose, and allowed me to make something positive out of this life-changing loss. I completed my thesis and presented it at my university. It was incredibly empowering."

Be open to communicating with others about what you do and do not need. It can be hard for them to know unless you communicate directly.

"Some people showed they understood by respecting what I had told them to do, sometimes because they asked, and sometimes not."

> Move away from those who are not supportive.

"Even hanging out with people who are my friends could be very painful because of how obviously they did not understand what I was going through, and some were so uncomfortable they couldn't even look me in the eye when I was upset. As painful as that was to experience, I knew I was helping to make my days slightly better when I decided to stop spending time with people if after I parted company with them I actually felt worse than I had before I saw them, which was already pretty bad."

> Have a little fun. Do something to make you laugh and/or smile. Many may find this difficult to do at first, but it is wonderful medicine for the grieving soul.

"My roommate took the day off on the anniversary of my mom's passing and spent the day with me, doing things that made me think of my mom in a positive way, like going to the mall and trying on the ugliest dresses we could, something my mom and I used to do."

Although not illustrated by specific quotes, our authors also indicated the following messages through their stories:

- Work to resist the temptation to use alcohol or drugs to help with your coping. These can interfere with the grieving process or cover it up.

- Focus on your health. Grief can be a great stress on your body and mind. It can upset sleep patterns, lead to depression, weaken your immune system, and highlight medical problems. See your doctor if you are worried about your health-related symptoms.

Keep in mind that there is a national network of grieving college students, young adults, and supporters in the U.S. through the AMF Support Network (www.studentsofamf.org). Also, the boundaries of nationality are fluid in our digital world. AMF is open to establishing international chapters.

CHAPTER 14

Tips for Supporting Grieving College Students and Young Adults

To begin, we would like to thank you! You have chosen to read this book in order to help grieving college students and young adults. This step is so important and one that we hope many others will take too, to improve the experience of grief for young adults. By reading the narratives in this book and considering the reflection questions, we hope that you will be able to offer the high quality support that you wish to provide. We know it will mean a great deal to the grieving college students and young adults you seek to support.

In this chapter, we provide a list of suggestions for those who seek to offer support to grieving college students and young adults (e.g., non-grieving peers, parents, counselors). We have separated the chapter into general tips for supporters and a few additional specific tips for parents, non-grieving peers, counselors, college personnel and professors, and support group leaders. Using a similar format to Chapter 13, we provide a brief description of each suggestion followed by quote(s) from the authors to help illustrate the "lived" experience of each of these ideas. These suggestions are tips that grieving students themselves have offered. Some of these suggestions were reported by many, whereas others were only noted by a few. Please view these ideas as possibilities and be sure to personally evaluate how well each may or may not fit for you.

General Tips for Being Supportive to Grieving College Students and Young Adults

Display empathy rather than sympathy and acknowledge the depth of grief. Remain open to hearing about all aspects of his or her grief without pitying the grieving person.

"Empathy (giving and receiving) has definitely been the best medicine for me. While I was feeling lost and alone in high school, my history teacher, a man of very few emotions, came up to me about a week after my dad had died, and just said, 'My mom died when I was 17, too.' That was it, but that one line from that one stoic man made me realize that I was not the first person to experience this awful thing. I was not alone, even if I felt like I was."

"He didn't try to understand. He explained that he couldn't. But he helped me find a way to express my grief in my schoolwork. And he never shied away from my crying. It didn't surprise him or make him uncomfortable."

Keep the support going. Grief does not end and it is not a linear process. Avoid implying a timeline for grief.

"Ultimately, it boils down to empathy. Some in my life possessed that capacity to recognize the diversity of emotions, pain, and emptiness I felt. A select few were able to braid their empathy with compassion. And even fewer were able to maintain this empathy over time—long past the expiration date that others in my life had stamped on my grief."

"I really just wanted someone to sit with me and say, 'You know what? You're right, it sucks and I hate that you have to go through this. But, I'm here for you, and I'll still be here for you when you want to cry or when you're angry. If you need to yell about it to feel better, I'm here. If you want to vent, I'm here. And, if you need a laugh, I'm here. I may not understand what you're going through, but I'm here to listen, and I'll still be here days or years from now.'"

Be present and offer tangible and practical support when appropriate. Avoid giving specific advice, trying to "fix them," or trying to make it all better. Avoid making statements that begin with "You should" or "You will." These statements are too directive. Instead you could begin your comments with: "Have you thought about…" or "You might…"

"Even if it was only in my head, I never felt like my aunts *fully* understood how I felt, but they told me (and followed through) with their promise: 'Since you have no more dad, we will be there.' And they were. They came over every single day to cook for us, watch movies with us, be with us. To make sure the house didn't feel empty. One aunt even moved into our house for that reason, increasing her daily commute from 20 minutes to two hours, just to help out with keeping our lives as normal as possible. And even though their care did not feel the same way that empathy does, their unwavering and endless support of me and my sister, and the very noticeable amount that they increased their presence in our lives, did make me feel better, more loved, less lost."

"I would be so upset that I had not even noticed that as I talked she had not only been listening, but had also been doing huge amounts of dishes that had been piling up. I feel bad when other people have to clean up my messes, but when I apologized and tried to stop her (sometimes when she was mostly done), she would insist that all was well and joked that she thoroughly enjoyed mindless tasks that she can excel at, like doing dishes."

"People would tell me that they are there for me, but wouldn't show it in their *actions*. For a long time, I blamed everyone in my life for not showing that they care. Many people wrote on my

Facebook and texted me the first few months, but no one knew me well enough to know I am not one to reach out for help. Them telling me that they are there for me and are here to listen did not help me, as those were just words in a message."

Be open to the topic of grief and try not to avoid it. You may think that avoiding the topic is saving the griever from pain, but actually such avoidance can add to their pain. They are thinking about their grief, so when you bring it up you are likely opening an important window that will allow them to share.

"Unfortunately, there were a lot of people who were not supportive or helpful. Most people just have no idea how to handle such pain and grief. They are afraid of getting too close, of asking too many questions, of making it worse. But really, when your parent dies it can't get any worse. It is already the worst thing you can ever imagine, so asking a friend how they are coping will not make it worse. Remaining silent is the worst path to take because it increases the isolation of the survivor. Ask questions. Give hugs often. Remember important dates. Acknowledge how difficult holidays and birthdays are. These are all things I wish people had done for me, and wish people continued to do today."

"When I was coping with my mom's death, I didn't feel like I had any support from my family. What I wanted more than anything in the world was to be able to talk about my mom; her likes, her dislikes, memories, essentially anything and everything about her. I wanted assurance that although she was gone from the physical world, her memory and presence on my family wouldn't disappear as well. I now understand that it was never my family's intention to make me feel as though I couldn't turn to them."

"Even my own friends didn't know how to comfort me. I felt misunderstood, alone, and as if people didn't really care. When I was with my friends, we talked about other things, as if I hadn't just gone through such a big life-changing event. I think this contributed to me downplaying the whole situation, thinking it wasn't such a big deal and that I was fine."

Provide opportunities for genuine expression of grief without judging. Allow for the expression of negative emotions and be able sit with them—with the griever and with his or her challenging feelings. You do not need to feel pressure to "fix" their feelings.

"I also didn't feel like my friends or boyfriend got it, but they provided me a safe space to 'be me' and cry if I needed to, or get an extra hug."

"This friend, though he was no expert on grief either, just said to me as we were sitting down to dinner, 'OK. I want to hear it all.' It felt so liberating to have him invite me to share anything I wanted."

"Also, I felt pressured knowing that most people wanted me to respond in a positive way. People wanted to know that I was doing OK—that I was good even. It was as if they needed the reassurance that I was OK so they too could feel OK about the fact that their lives had not stopped in the same way mine had. So, instead of hearing how I actually felt, most people heard a lie. The people who asked, 'How are you holding up?' typically received the more honest answer because I felt as if they had already accepted that my response might be negative or pessimistic, yet were ready to hear it."

"I hate it when people would try to cheer me up, because although driven by affection and goodwill, people doing that made me feel like they did not understand that sadness, pain, frustration, and other 'negative' feelings are just as much a part of life as the 'positive' ones, and acting like feeling that way was a choice did not acknowledge that they are real feelings and if ignored, they do not go away but wreak havoc by being contained."

Ask about the loved one(s) who died. Display your interest in learning about that person with questions, such as "Tell me something special about your deceased loved one."

"I loved when people presented me with an opportunity to talk about my dad. My favorite thing was, and still is, when people share their memories of him. Although it can be bittersweet at times, sharing memories not only helps me remember him and learn new things about him, but it also gives me the chance to talk."

"Many people assume it is too painful to talk about and don't want to make you upset. But I yearned for people to ask about him. She also asked when he died and when his birthday was and continues to check in with me on those days. I don't think any of my best friends even know these dates, and this means a tremendous amount to me. She still acknowledges how hard it is and understands how big of a deal it was and is for me to talk about him. Recently, I posted a picture of my dad and me on Facebook for the first time, and she told me how proud she was of me."

Consider your own strengths and relationship with the college student who is grieving—what can you uniquely offer?

"At my dad's funeral, my aunt's (dad's sister) ex-husband came unexpectedly. He scooped me up into perhaps the best hug I've ever gotten—one that told me, without any words, that he knew what I was feeling (his mom had died when he was a toddler), that he was here (even if he didn't have to be), and that everything would be OK. That hug gave me more comfort than all the other people who showed up, and all the cards and flowers that we got."

"My younger cousin, who was maybe in middle school, decided to write me a rap. It said he couldn't know how I felt, but that he was here for me. I remember appreciating getting that from such a young kid, who could still tap into how much I was hurting."

"So it may sound silly, but I was incredibly touched that for our first time catching up in person since my brother died, she arrived not even one minute late, despite her difficulties doing so normally, and the incredibly awful way she felt. Knowing her, that action told me how much she cared to be there for me, which was in and of itself able to make me feel quite supported."

Be open to the uniqueness of grief and acknowledge that uniqueness, rather than sending messages that there is one right way to grieve or implying that you know more about their grief than they do.

"She knows that we have different religious views and beliefs, and one of the things I particularly appreciated was more of something she *did not do* than something she did. From the first moment after my brother died, she managed to listen to me and be there for me in a way that was totally respectful of our different beliefs, and though I'm sure she prayed for me and on the inside was wishing that I would welcome God and realize his presence in my life, not once did she say that out loud."

Avoid comments and statements that imply judgment, minimize the griever's experience, or attempt to placate.

"Then there were those who made 'The Comments.' The Comments are those that will forever be etched in my mind. 'Why aren't you crying?' my classmate asked during art class just nine days after his death. 'If my dad died, I'd be crying. I love my dad.' 'You can't keep using this [being upset about my dad's death] as an excuse forever,' said a friend several years after my dad's death. The list goes on and on."

"To me the people who seemed not to 'get it' are the ones who said they knew *exactly* what I was going through because their boyfriend had broken up with them, their parents were divorced, their pet had died, they had failed a test, etc. While I am not one who likes to compare losses, since each loss is unique, I knew that they truly had no idea how I was feeling."

"Similarly, I was never a fan of the commonplace 'he's in a better place' or 'God has a plan' sentiments. I didn't always want to hear about how it would get better, nor did I want to hear about the silver lining or light at the end of the tunnel. My thoughts were simple: I don't care *whose* plan it is, I don't like this plan, and it would be better if my dad were still with me, here, on Earth, physically."

"One of the most frustrating attempts at helping was the constant 'it will get better!' or 'he'll fight this and win!' language from some people in my life. I always found the battlefield language of cancer diagnosis exhausting. The notion that we were in the midst of war was never a helpful (or relatable) analogy, and the idea of winning was far from my mind. Similarly, though hope was welcome, blind optimism was aggravating. I understood the sentiment beneath it, but it was jarring to hear so much positivity after a bad diagnosis."

Recognize and communicate the fact that grief does not end. In the words of Keanu Reeves: "Grief does not end—it changes shape."

"One day I was having a 'dad moment' and feeling nostalgic when my dad's best friend donated to a charity cause of mine and told me that my dad would have been proud. That friend showed his continued love of my dad through loving me and my sister. I cried as I was happily telling a good friend this. He answered,

'Uh, it's been over ten years. Why are you still crying? Shouldn't you be over it by now?' I explained to him that the pain is like a wound and a scar. With time, the wound is not fresh and biting, but if you push on a scar—like if your dad's best friend tells you that your dad would've been so proud of you—it will still hurt somewhere inside. Not a surface wound, but something below, a reminder of the original injury. He didn't get it, and continued saying he was shocked I was still crying."

"One of the most insensitive, unhelpful responses to my grief process actually came from one of my professors. After two weeks of falling behind on my assignments, I decided to confide in him about the root of my difficulties. 'My dad died less than a year ago and I am still having a very hard time.' I was not looking for special treatment or leniency in any way, just compassion from one human being to another. Instead, I was met with, 'Less than a *year* ago? Shouldn't you be over that by now?' I stood there, frozen, ears ringing from the thoughtlessness. I wanted to yell back at him, 'No, I'm not over that now and I probably will not be "over that" ever.' Years later, his response is still burned into my memory."

Be consistent and persistent in your messages of care and concern. They don't have to be huge gestures.

"I began to ignore most calls or texts, yet one friend persisted, keeping calling or texting occasionally throughout the whole year. Even though I rarely responded, it was surprising how touched I was that he kept on trying, even though I rebuffed his attempts to stay in touch—simply knowing that someone was thinking about my family was more meaningful that I thought it would be."

"One thing that has helped since has been when very close friends of mine call me on the annual date just to let me know they are thinking about me. I believe that helps me process my grief much more than they think."

Although not illustrated by specific quotes, our authors also indicated the following messages through their stories:

- Encourage your loved one to reach out to others for support too.

- Encourage your loved one to consider memorializing their loved one by participating in community service and pledge to participate along with them.

- Avoid making assumptions that someone is doing great and "all better" based on their outward appearances—grieving is an internal process (e.g., feelings, body sensations, and other individual differences) that may never be seen.

- If the grieving college student or young adult is suicidal, it is your moral and ethical responsibility to find/refer him or her to a mental health professional. (In the U.S. through campus directory, calling the National Suicide Prevention Hotline (U.S.): 1-800-273-8255 or the Samaritans (U.K.): 08457 909090, calling 911/999, or http://locator.apa.org.)

Additional Specific Tips for a Parent who Wants to be Supportive

Acknowledge the depth and uniqueness of grief.

"Of all the big and little shows of sympathy, empathy, and care, my mom's understanding and true 'getting it' about the effect on my own life was the biggest."

Be open to talking about your own grief, but also be clear that you are still the parent and will continue to be in your child's life.

"She kept up her 'brave face' and not once cried in front of my sister and me. She refused to let us stay home longer than a week to wallow, and insisted on us going to school, playing volleyball, studying, seeing friends. Life HAD to continue, she wouldn't have let it be any other way. I never saw it, because she did it so well, hid her immense pain, through daily emails to my dad's account and secretly seeing a therapist to help her air out her own grief. She still never missed a volleyball game and made sure that we didn't either. Because of all that she endured, silently and without my knowing, and all that she sacrificed, my life was able to continue on, and my grieving process was able to get the healthiest start it could have. She 'got it'—the impact of losing my dad—more than anyone else, because it affected her most, and yet she was able to channel all of that immense scary stuff to ensure that my life would continue on as normally as possible. From the moment she left my dad at the hospital, she became both a mom and a dad, and understood how to best help me grieve, heal, and grow."

Additional Specific Tips for Non-Grieving Peers who Want to be Supportive

Work to avoid taking your own parents/siblings for granted— particularly in front of bereaved peers.

"People who would be taking their dads for granted and complaining in front of me really made me upset."

Be trustworthy and respectful.

"She was someone I considered my 'best friend.' I realized after about a year that I had put my trust in the wrong person; not only was she judgmental, but she was not someone who uplifted me and she caused me to be mad at her very often. She shared very personal information about me with others, didn't respect me and my time or privacy, and did many things that hurt me badly."

Risk getting involved and reaching out to and supporting bereaved peers.

"The night my father died my mom suggested I call my closest friends and tell them the news. One of the girls insisted on coming over that night, even though it was after 11pm. I waited for her on the front steps of my house. I do not know why I was so eager to see her that night. The moment she hugged me I fell apart again, an instance that was to happen too many times over the following weeks. She stayed at my house with her dad until 1am. It meant the world to see a friend care so much. At school the next day she had all my teachers sign a card for me. It made it easier for me to know I had her to help me through my days at school when I was away from my mom. I can never thank her enough for coming to my house that night and for being there with me when I needed her the most."

Additional Specific Tips for Counselors who Want to be Supportive

Be genuine and real and work to build a strong alliance.

"I began the first session stating, 'Please don't ever ask me how something makes me feel.' He laughed, as he often did at me, and that is exactly what I needed. One day he asked me why I had such a difficult time talking to my friends about my dad. I responded simply, stating, 'I don't want to make other people sad.' Once again he laughed and stated, 'Well, you need to get over that.'"

"The open and frank conversation that we had was the first chance I had really gotten to open up about my experience, and the way he shared his own experience with his dad's death (he was only a bit older than I was when my dad died) helped validate my feelings and helped me understand that I was not alone."

Become familiar with the current grief theories that emphasize the dynamic and idiosyncratic elements of the grieving process. Avoid the use of stage theories and offer psychoeducational information to grieving students.

"The counselor told me I was in the 'denial' stage as I explained that, sometimes, I would expect to see him or get a phone call from him. I was not in denial. I had prepared his funeral, stood at his open casket, packed all of his earthly possessions. I just desperately missed him. I didn't want to be categorized, especially with categories that didn't fit."

"I think some more grief education would be helpful so that the students experiencing grief know they are not alone. Some education all around on grief would also be helpful so friends, teacher, counselors, and coaches would be more understanding and would be able to accommodate students with grief more effectively."

Allow space for nonjudgmental sharing.

"She never judged me and encouraged me to say whatever I wanted or needed to say. She helped me heal in ways that I never could have done by myself."

"He told me that I struck him as one of those Wall Street types. Someone who, given a real vacation, wouldn't know what to do with herself and would inevitably be bored within hours. A real 'control freak.' I felt myself closing down inside. I was so filled with anger toward this man, I stopped the session early, canceled all my appointments, and never looked back. I realize now that this counseling student was probably doing the best he could. I recognize that not all counselors are so harsh or quick to judge, some are still just learning, the same way I am still learning."

"I sought counseling from campus psychological services. I felt my counselor was more interested in discovering why I was feeling my emotions at a time when I couldn't fully describe them to myself. I had wanted the counselor to help me direct and sort out my thoughts but in the end we had different goals for my grief therapy and so I discontinued with it."

Allow for the processing of deep emotions and the expression of blame.

"The first year after my loss, I started seeing a spiritual counselor. She taught me affirmations and helped me see that we are not our thoughts or bodies. This was helpful in understanding that I had strong emotions but was disconnected. I felt very guilty and felt inhuman for not missing my sister and for not knowing how to connect with my parents, who were hurting. But with her help, I was able to stop blaming myself so much and begin to understand the impact my sister's death had on me. I still see her every once in a while, and she has been there to witness my transformation."

Follow through on commitments.

"I found that the counseling center on campus was the least helpful during my grief journey. I was told that there would be a support group starting 'soon' and that they would contact me when it started. I never heard anything from them again."

Realize the power of peer support for grieving students and be an advocate for such opportunities on your campus.

"Peer-led support groups are a great option for those students like me who did not want to seek counseling. This group creates a community atmosphere within a community that seems to ignore any real problems. It allows you to be serious and talk about what is happening and how you feel in a college atmosphere, one in which you are trying to find yourself and have a good time. It creates a connection with people so you are not so isolated."

Additional Specific Tips for College Personnel and Professors who Want to be Supportive

Allow time for being present and letting grieving students vent even in the midst of the busy college environment. Making such time is perhaps particularly important in the college environment as grief is counter to the usual focus on growth, learning, and fun.

"One of those advisors already knew me quite well from what I had gone through the year before, and she again proved to be a great resource to have, because although I almost never asked her to step in to ask my profs for extensions or anything, I could vent to her—an adult, who was not part of my social circle but knew the way that the environment I was in worked, and had to keep my experiences confidential."

"But my other close friends were not in my peer group at all—our Director of Admissions and my Women's Studies professor. Both of them became endless sources of light, wisdom, laughter, and compassion. They balanced conversations about the latest *Glee* episode with a discussion of chemo cocktails. It normalized everything."

Work hard to remember or keep track when students share with you about their death losses, even if you have a large number of students.

"From his response he had entirely forgotten the conversation we had had a couple weeks before where I told him what I was going through and that I didn't expect extensions but I might not be on the ball always and I would keep him in the loop. I was hurt and frustrated and mad that he did not make the effort to remember who I was after that, especially since our class was only seminar-sized and because he had asked me very personal questions about my grief and how I was doing and if I should be in school at all. I appreciated him asking the difficult questions at the time, in case no one else had, but the fact that he did not remember my answers was not well received."

Offer reasonable accommodations when possible (e.g., late assignments, incompletes).

"For the most part, my professors were incredibly helpful, supportive, and understanding. I came in during office hours for extra tutoring, took exams at different times and got notes from classmates. I only experienced one professor who made me doubt the system. He had given me a hard time occasionally for missing so much class and having to retake tests. There was little to no empathy in his voice when discussing the time I had been absent.

I tried to be understanding. I'm sure he'd heard every excuse in the book and had to be cautious of the students who would take advantage of any ounce of leniency. However, the moment that crossed the line for me was when I had sent an email to him, explaining that my father had passed and I would be away for three days for the services. I received an email from his secretary, requesting my father's obituary. I was shocked."

"I have had teachers in the past who brushed off the fact that I was going through grief... Academically, I struggled being able to stay focused... Even though I had forewarned my professors of what had happened on Christmas Eve, they would see me skipping class as being lazy or a poor student. Little do they know, the night before I cried for hours, stared at the same page of my biology book until the library closed, and then laid wide awake until the morning came. My professor offered extra time on one quiz if needed, however, in the end he was the most disappointing professor. After working through the hardest semester of my life and temporarily taking time off soccer to focus on my studies and myself I missed the grade needed to move on. Because I was a few points off from this cutoff, a waiver exists that professors could sign students through. When contacted, his response via email was:

> I reviewed your scores in Gen Bio 2 and spent some time thinking about signing your waiver. Unfortunately, I cannot support the waiver. I know that you had other factors such as soccer that consumed a lot of your time, but I don't feel you mastered the material at a level necessary to succeed in Genetics and Microbiology—they are tougher courses. I feel it is best for you to retake Gen Bio 2 this fall and focus on improving your study skills, time management, and understanding the course content.

There are a few things wrong with this statement. Although I don't think that it is right to use grief as a crutch to coast through life, I do think that in some cases that it should be considered."

Advocate for the needs of grieving students through the development of campus policies and encouragement of support groups for grieving students (e.g., AMF Support Network; www.studentsofamf.org).

"I was surprised that even though it was a religious-based college, there was nothing offering grief support/counseling. This was a struggle for me to find a safe place to work through my grief."

Train Resident Advisors (RAs) about grief—they have daily contact with students.

"When I entered college, I had an RA my freshman year who was very sweet and reached out to me a few times. I never shared my 'secret' with her or opened up, but I knew she cared about me, and that was comforting through such hard times."

Be approachable.

"On top of that, I was getting Bs in my classes for the first time, despite my continued efforts. My professor didn't understand; I didn't know how to tell them about this, or if they would care."

Work to create a supportive campus environment—where people reach out to each other.

"I had the biggest problem trying to explain to my peers how I felt. Part of the culture of this campus fosters a lot of self-first mentality, where others don't take the time to show a particularly deep level of empathy for other people's problems. Most people that I tried to talk to about the way I felt didn't have any sort of basis for understanding as significant of a loss as I had suffered."

"It would have been helpful if information was somehow shared with professors and advisors. If a student can identify one staff member they feel comfortable talking with, this person should assist with talking to professors. I never wanted it to seem like I was making excuses or wanted special treatment, but there were several times when I was seriously depressed and academically suffered because of it. I also think the counseling centers could be more proactive about being involved academically. It would of course require the student's permission, but having an advocate to talk to professors would have taken the burden off having to tell them myself. I would have welcomed that, but at Georgetown the counseling center is technically a separate entity from the university. So when the option was to tell professors myself or not tell them at all, it was not a hard decision to keep everything to myself. Finally, grief is not an emotion embraced in most college environments, which is a more universal problem to be addressed by administrators and professors. Staff members could make it clear at freshman orientation or at the start of their class that emotional issues are common and frequent among college students, and to not be afraid to come forward with challenges and struggles."

Additional Specific Tips for Support Group Leaders who Want to be Supportive

Realize that a formal structure is likely not necessary. Flexibility is critical and the power of the group is in the members' connections with one another.

"There was almost no formal structure, we led the conversations ourselves, no one was forced beyond their comfort zone in divulging any details they did not want to, and we ended every time with hugs all around. I am a big fan of hugs. Getting to know the other group members was a very powerful experience, and we supported each other both in those meetings and beyond. Even knowing that some of the other faces in the crowds on campus understood quite a bit of what I was going through was very valuable and comforting to me."

Involve non-bereaved peers when appropriate.

"Once a semester, we had 'bring a friend to support group' night, where each person in the group brought a friend who was not grieving a loss and did not have a sick parent or family member. This was a really helpful meeting because we discussed how our friends who couldn't relate to exactly what we were going through could be supportive. I found out that my close friend wanted to help and was curious about how my dad was doing, but was often afraid to bring up the topic of my dad's illness for fear of upsetting me by reminding me of it. To be able to address issues like this made it easier to get support—and more importantly, learn how to ask for help."

Consider the idea of weekend retreats away from campus.

"The summer before I began graduate school, when I was 24, I was fortunate enough to participate in a weekend camp for young adults with Comfort Zone Camp. The comprehensive weekend retreat offered a protective, intensive, 'bubble' (as they call it), where I had the time to open up in an environment that was both safe and full of understanding people. Though it is not an inexpensive resource, I think it would be great if universities offered similar retreat opportunities for grieving college students. The opportunity to get away from campus and create a safe environment was essential for me to feel comfortable enough to take my grief journey to the next level, which I did by sharing more details of my grief story than I have ever done previously."

Allow time for non-grief conversations.

"The peer support group was definitely the most meaningful to me during my grief journey. I have been to therapists several times, and while they serve a purpose, even they could not connect to me in the same way the group members could. Student-led support groups are inclusive, flexible, cohesive, and accepting. We could end up talking about one topic for the whole meeting, such as the holidays or when your remaining parent started dating again. Or we would float between a variety of topics. One of my most memorable meetings was when we spent nearly the whole meeting talking about the Borat movie, laughing hysterically and just feeling normal for a while. I liked the flexibility of it being student-run, because if no one felt like being serious we could just laugh and joke for a meeting. But that rarely happened, because the support group was the one safe space most of us would talk about our parents and our experience and we valued it highly."

AUTHOR BACKGROUND INFORMATION

Author background information is given in the table on the following pages.

Name	Sex	Age	Death loss	Cause of death	Time since death loss	College timing	Ethnicity	Page
Tiffany	Female	28	Father	Aneurysm	11 years, 2 months	Prior	Asian American	19
Ashley	Female	27	Father	Cancer	7 years, 4 months	During	Caucasian	25
Michelle	Female	26	Older brother and father	Suicide/schizophrenia and mesothelioma	8 years and 12 years	Prior	Caucasian	28
Kristen S.	Female	23	Mother	Suicide/bipolar disorder	6 years, 6 months	Prior	Caucasian	35
Carolyn	Female	24	Younger sister	Sudden/unclear cause	3 years, 5 months	During	Caucasian	41
Allison	Female	24	Mother	Scleroderma	11 years, 1 month	Prior	Caucasian	44
Casey	Female	25	Father	Colorectal cancer	3 years, 2 months	Sick prior, died during	Caucasian	51

						Sick prior, died during		
Patrick	Male	21	Mother	Amyotrophic lateral sclerosis	1 year, 10 months		Asian American/ Caucasian	58
Patricia	Female	29	Father	Heart attack	8 years, 11 months	During	Caucasian	62
Margaret	Female	28	Mother	Cancer	2 years, 2 months	After	Caucasian	67
Alex	Female	20	Father	Heart attack	2 years	During	Asian American	72
Danielle B.	Female	23	Father	Diabetes— extended complications	9 years, 3 months	Prior	Caucasian/ Jewish	76
Katie	Female	22	Older brother	Drowned during seizure	1 year, 4 months	During	Caucasian	82
Samantha	Female	21	Father	Septic shock after gastric bypass surgery	10 years	Prior	Caucasian	86
Sarah	Female	23	Mother	Breast cancer	2 years, 8 months	During	Caucasian	94

Name	Sex	Age	Death loss	Cause of death	Time since death loss	College timing	Ethnicity	Page
Kate	Female	27	Younger sister and mother	Neuroblastoma and glioblastoma	12 years, 4 months and 11 years, 9 months	Prior	Asian American and Caucasian	99
Julie	Female	26	Father	Amyotrophic lateral sclerosis	3 years, 7 months	Sick prior, died soon after	Caucasian	103
Charlene	Female	28	Father	Glioblastoma multiforme cancer	5 years, 3 months	During	Caucasian	110
Kristen W.	Female	25	Mother	Breast cancer	9 years, 3 months	Prior	Caucasian	112
Shirin	Female	21	Older sister	Car accident	4 years, 2 months	Prior	Arab-Amercian	116
Katherine	Female	26	Father	Liver failure	11 years, 6 months	Prior	Caucasian	122
Brent	Male	27	Father	Heart attack	15 years	Prior	Caucasian	127
Danielle C.	Female	23	Father	Brain cancer	3 years, 7 months	During	Caucasian	131

Name	Sex	Age	Parent	Cause of death	Time	Timing	Ethnicity	Page
Kaitlyn	Female	22	Father	Heart attack	10 years, 8 months	Prior	Caucasian	134
Leah	Female	22	Father	Heart attack	3 years, 10 months	Prior	Caucasian	138
Alyssa	Female	23	Father	Heart attack	3 years, 8 months	During	Caucasian	144
Mary	Female	23	Mother	Metastatic breast cancer	4 years, 9 months	During	Caucasian	147
Loreal	Female	21	Mother	Diving accident	4 years, 6 months	Prior	Asian American	148
Isabel	Female	24	Father	Hemorrhagic stroke	3 years, 11 months	During	Caucasian	154
Bethany	Female	28	Mother	Ovarian cancer	6 years	During	Caucasian	156
Jeffrey	Male	26	Father	Car accident	5 years, 9 months	During	Caucasian	157
Meghan Rizon	Female	21	Mother	Breast cancer	3 years, 1 month	Prior	Caucasian	162
Na Hyung	Female	22	Mother	Cancer	4 years, 1 month	Prior	Asian American	165

REFERENCES

Arnett, J. J. (2004) *Emerging Adulthood: The Winding Road from the Late Teens through the Twenties.* New York, NY: Oxford University Press.

Balk, D. E., Walker, A. C., and Baker, A. (2010) "Prevalence and severity of college student bereavement examined in a randomly selected sample." *Death Studies 34*, 5, 459–468.

Center for Complicated Grief (2014) *What is complicated grief.* Accessed on December 15, 2014 at www.complicatedgrief.org/bereavement.

Doka, K. J. and Martin, T. (2010) *Grieving Beyond Gender: Understanding the Ways Men and Women Mourn.* New York, NY: Routledge.

DuBois, D. L., Portillo, N., Rhodes, J. E., Silverthorn, N., and Valentine, J. C. (2011) "How effective are mentoring programs for youth? A systematic assessment of the evidence." *Psychological Science in the Public Interest 12*, 2, 57–91.

Klass, D., Silverman, P. R., and Nickman, S. (eds) (1996) *Continuing Bonds: New Understandings of Grief.* New York, NY: Taylor & Francis.

Kuntz, B. (1991) "Exploring the grief of adolescents after the death of a parent." *Journal of Child and Adolescent Psychiatric Nursing 4*, 3, 105–109.

Neimeyer, R. A. (2001) "Reauthoring life narratives: Grief therapy as meaning reconstruction." *Israel Journal of Psychiatry and Related Sciences 38*, 3–4, 171–183.

Parkes, C. M. and Prigerson. H. G. (2009) *Bereavement: Studies of Grief in Adult Life.* New York, NY: Routledge.

Shear, K. and Shair, H. (2005) "Attachment, loss, and complicated grief." *Developmental Psychology 47*, 253–267.

Straker, N. (2013) "The Avoidance of Facing Death: Its Consequences to our Patients, Families, Medical Students, and Young Physicians." In N. Straker (ed.) *Facing Cancer and the Fear of Death: A Psychoanalytic Perspective on Treatment.* Lanham, MD: Jason Aronson.

Stroebe, M. S., Hansson, R. O., Schut, H., and Stroebe, W. (eds) (2008) *Handbook of Bereavement Research and Practice: Advances in Theory and Intervention.* Washington, DC: American Psychological Association.

Walsh, F. and McGoldrick, M. (2004) *Living Beyond Loss: Death in the Family.* New York, NY: Norton.

Wilder, T. (1927, 2002) *The Bridge of San Luis Rey.* New York, NY: HarperCollins.